The Prince George's County Historical Society is pleased to present to the citizens of our county this Tricentennial edition of Prince George's County: A Pictorial History by Alan Virta.

This publication was made possible through the assistance of the following organizations:

The Aman Memorial Trust
The Gilbert and Jaylee Mead Family Foundation
Preservation Maryland
Prince George's Heritage, Inc.

The Society gratefully acknowledges their support.

This beautifully illustrated volume is sure to be treasured for generations to come.

Historic Marietta at Glenn Dale, Maryland

Headquarters of the **Prince George's County Historical Society**

PRINCE GEORGE'S COUNTY

A Pictorial History

BY ALAN VIRTA

The Donning Company/Publishers
Design by W. Bradley Miller

Mrs. Hermine Johnston offered a wide range of food and dry goods in her store in Bowie early in the twentieth century. General stores like this one were important social and business centers in old Prince George's County. Mrs. Johnston's store was located near the railroad tracks in that part of town now known as "old Bowie." Courtesy of Thelma Brady Gasch and the Belair Stables Museum

To my parents

CONTENTS

Overleaf:
Boy Scouts study a map, about 1935.
Their leader was Robert E. Ennis of
Capitol Heights. Courtesy of Blanche L.
Ennis

FOREWORD

When the Donning Company originally contacted us in 1982 concerning a pictorial history of Prince George's County, we were delighted to encourage their interest. Although Prince George's County dates from the seventeenth century and possesses a heritage which can be matched by few other counties, little of a formal nature had been written of its total history.

The basic general references on the county were three in number: Effie Gwynn Bowie's *Across the Years in Prince George's County* (1947), primarily a genealogical work on the early families but filled with historical facts; Louise Joyner Hienton's *Prince George's Heritage* (1972), a scholarly study from 1696 through the end of the eighteenth century; and Judge R. Lee Van Horn's *Out of The Past: Prince Georgeans and Their Land* (1976), a down-to-earth report of everyday life in the county as taken from the public records and newspapers through the beginning of the Civil War.

When questioned back then as to a potential author, one name immediately came to mind—that of Alan Virta. In 1974, as a recent Phi Beta Kappa graduate in history from the University of Maryland, he had volunteered to edit the monthly newsletter of the Prince George's County Historical Society. During the intervening years the material he produced on almost every facet of county history brought acclaim from members of the society and professional historians alike. In addition to his editorial work, Alan Virta was active in historic preservation, serving as the first chairman of the Historic Preservation Commission of Prince George's County.

The first edition of the present volume, which appeared during Maryland's 350th anniversary year, was the first major work to deal with the full sweep of county history, from its erection on Saint George's Day, 1696, to the present era. As such, it was destined to join the aforementioned classics as a reference on county life.

In the introductory essays to each chapter, as well as in the captions and photographic images, Mr. Virta captured a feeling for the quality of life in Prince George's County, from colonial times through revolution, British invasion, civil war, postwar depression, streetcar suburbia, world war, and massive development.

And, since its publication in 1984, *Prince George's County: A Pictorial History* has been accepted as the primary single reference on the fascinating chronicle of county life and development over almost three centuries. The limited printing of the first edition and public demand have dictated the appearance of this second edition with updated material, under the sponsorship of the Prince George's County Historical Society. And, once again author Alan Virta has captured the diversified events of an additional era—the eighties—with his talented pen.

In five short years, during 1996, we will celebrate the Tricentennial of Prince George's County. May the record of the past, as contained in these pages, provide guidance and inspiration for direction in the fourth century. We pray that all of our citizens will join in this quest.

And, to the citizens of Prince George's County who will be inspired by this work, we extend a hearty and sincere invitation to join the Prince George's County Historical Society in its continuing efforts to collect and disseminate the evidence of our colorful present and past.

FOREWORD, 1998

Frederick S. DeMarr died on September 5, 1997. He devoted most of his time and energy to the preservation of the history of this county. His efforts were mainly channeled through the Prince George's County Historical Society and the library he founded. We therefore dedicate this book to the memory of Fred and repeat his invitation to everyone to join us in our continuing effort to collect and disseminate the evidence of our colorful present and past. This edition of *Prince George's County: A Pictorial History*, is written after we celebrated the Tricentennial of Prince George's County in 1996. It was a grand celebration in which a majority of the citizens participated. Mr. Virta once again has captured a feeling for the quality of life in our county as it was three hundred years ago as well as how it was celebrated when we began our fourth century of being Prince George's County.

Jane Eagen
President
Prince George's County Historical Society

*P*rince George's County was named for Prince George of Denmark, husband of England's Queen Anne. George was born in 1653, the second son of Denmark's King Frederick III. He and Anne were married in 1683, and at her accession to the throne in 1702 he was named generalissimo of the queen's forces and lord high admiral. He died in 1708. Anne later wrote of George, "You can judge the magnitude of our affection because such a husband was an inestimable treasure, who loved us with such tenderness for the course of so many years." Prince George never visited America, so he never saw the county that was named for him. This portrait was painted by Sir Godfrey Kneller. It is part of the collections of the National Maritime Museum, Greenwich, London. Courtesy of the Prince George's County Historical Society

PREFACE

Semper Eadem is the motto on the Great Seal of Prince George's County, Maryland. In Latin, it means "Ever the Same." Nothing could be further from the truth. Since its establishment in 1696, Prince George's County has led four very different lives. The first was that of the frontier, a land of opportunity; rough, raw, egalitarian. Out of that frontier evolved an ordered, conservative agricultural society, made rich by the cultivation of tobacco and the labor of slaves. The Civil War brought that society to an end, and for two generations, Prince George's County would rightly be described as a rural backwater, still agricultural and still conservative, but now impoverished; an inward-looking society of small farms and villages. Then, during the twentieth century, a dramatic transformation took place. The expansion of the federal workforce, the availability of the automobile, and the growth of the city of Washington beyond its bounds changed Prince George's County into a suburban county, a dynamic part of a great metropolitan era.

I grew up in the suburbs of Prince George's County during the 1950s and 1960s and witnessed many of the changes of the suburban era. My family's route to church in the fifties took us down Annapolis Road, past the great pillars of the Lanham mansion. The sight of that stately home, set well off the road at the head of a broad green lawn, conjured up images of another day and first set me to wondering about Prince George's County's past. The house is gone now, and Annapolis Road is a far cry from the tree-lined two lane highway of just a few decades ago. Such is change. It is my hope that this book, through its images of days past, will introduce others to Prince George's County's history and preserve, in some measure, Prince George's County's heritage.

Although my name appears on the title page, this book could not have been produced without the advice, assistance, and encouragement of many friends and colleagues. I am particularly indebted to the late Frederick S. DeMarr, president of the Prince George's County Historical Society, who first suggested that I undertake this project. His advice throughout was invaluable, for no one was more familiar with the fine details of county history than he.

The choice of photographs for a work such as this one is always a difficult task. There are simply more good photos than could be included in a single volume. Choosing photos to represent the county's historic homes was a particular problem; it would take an entire book to include them all. For representations of historic homes I relied heavily on the photographs of the Historic American Buildings Survey, a New Deal project of the 1930s. The HABS photos appear throughout the book, and are so identified wherever they occur.

The color photos in the third edition came from several sources, but mostly from the files of the Maryland-National Capital Park and Planning Commission and the *Prince George's Journal*, the county's daily newspaper. To Steven Abramowitz, photographer for the M-NCPPC, and to Lon Slepicka, Kathy Williams, and the photographers and officers of the *Journal*, I offer the warmest thanks.

My thanks are also extended to all the other individuals and institutions who provided photographs for this pictorial history. Their names appear with their photographs. There are a number of others whose names do not appear in the text, but whose assistance must be acknowledged nonetheless. They include librarians, archivists, historians, and friends, and their help is greatly appreciated.

Christopher N. Allan; Cathy Wallace Allen; Shirley Baltz; David J. Bohaska; Raymond W. Bellamy, Jr.; Theodore L. Bissell; Dennis Campbell; Mary Carter; Marcia Christensen; Betty R. Collinson; Margaret Cook; Susanna Cristofane; Sandra Cross; W. C. "Bud" Dutton, Jr.; Robert T. Ennis; Willard and Elaine Entwisle; Ann Ferguson; Brett W. Ferrigan; Richard Fisher; Bianca Floyd; Allan O. Hare, Jr.; Reverend Lawrence R. Harris, Jr.; Susan Helmann; Averil J. Kadis; Eleanora Bowling Kane; Mrs. Brooke Kerby; Lorenzo Long; Bernard G. Loveless; Margaret Mullikin Marshall; Joyce McDonald; Elizabeth Miller; Dorothy G. Moore; Matthew Neitzey; Kathy Peterson; Harry Price; Reverend Edward Raffetto; Ivan and Dorothy Rainwater; Robert D. Reed; Warren and Julie Rhoads; Gail C. Rothrock; Claudia J. Scott; James M. Sherwood; Mary Ternes; James H. Trimble; John M. Walton, Jr.; Sara Walton; Mame Warren; Lynda Hall Wynn; Margaret Yewell; and Anthony Zito.

Finally, special thanks must be extended to my parents and my brothers for their many favors, including the typing of most of the manuscript. And without the assistance of Susan Pearl in 1998, the preparation of a third edition in Boise, Idaho, would have been next to impossible.

Alan Virta
August 28, 1998

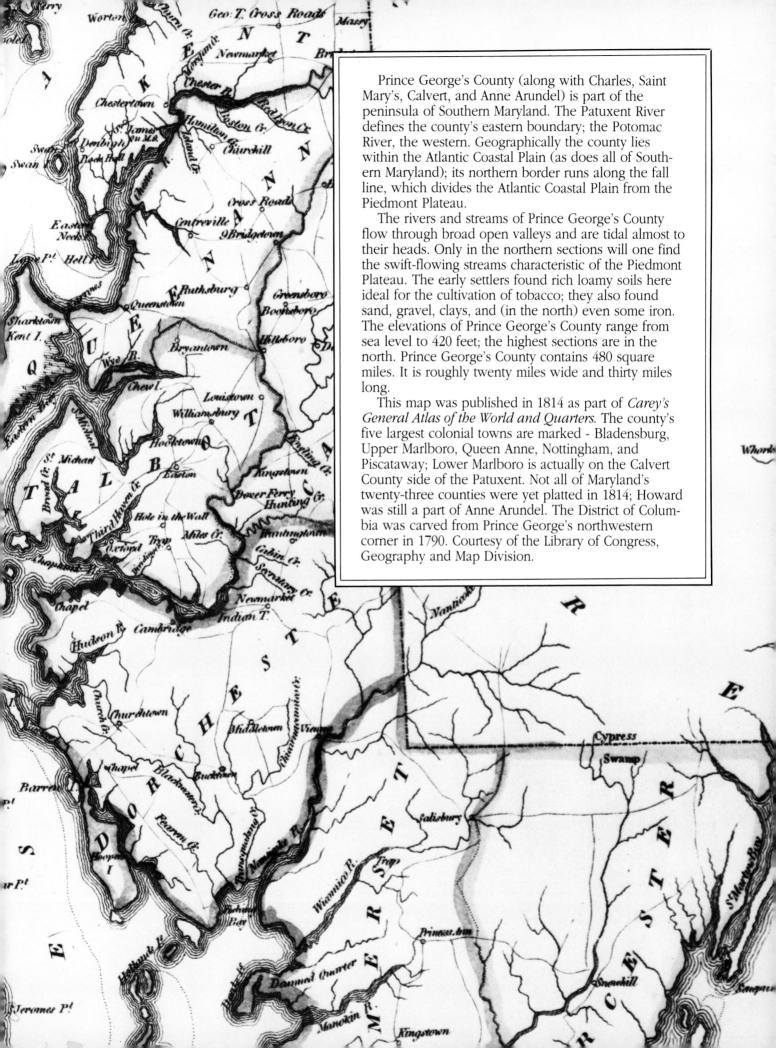

Prince George's County (along with Charles, Saint Mary's, Calvert, and Anne Arundel) is part of the peninsula of Southern Maryland. The Patuxent River defines the county's eastern boundary; the Potomac River, the western. Geographically the county lies within the Atlantic Coastal Plain (as does all of Southern Maryland); its northern border runs along the fall line, which divides the Atlantic Coastal Plain from the Piedmont Plateau.

The rivers and streams of Prince George's County flow through broad open valleys and are tidal almost to their heads. Only in the northern sections will one find the swift-flowing streams characteristic of the Piedmont Plateau. The early settlers found rich loamy soils here ideal for the cultivation of tobacco; they also found sand, gravel, clays, and (in the north) even some iron. The elevations of Prince George's County range from sea level to 420 feet; the highest sections are in the north. Prince George's County contains 480 square miles. It is roughly twenty miles wide and thirty miles long.

This map was published in 1814 as part of *Carey's General Atlas of the World and Quarters*. The county's five largest colonial towns are marked - Bladensburg, Upper Marlboro, Queen Anne, Nottingham, and Piscataway; Lower Marlboro is actually on the Calvert County side of the Patuxent. Not all of Maryland's twenty-three counties were yet platted in 1814; Howard was still a part of Anne Arundel. The District of Columbia was carved from Prince George's northwestern corner in 1790. Courtesy of the Library of Congress, Geography and Map Division.

Chapter
1

THE DELIGHTSOME LAND

The story of Prince George's County begins in the sixteenth and seventeenth centuries with the discovery and exploration of the Chesapeake Bay. Although the Spanish in the Caribbean knew of the bay, the English were the first to explore and chart it. What they found pleased them. Wrote Captain John Smith, the bay's first explorer: "Within is a country that may have the prerogative over the most places known, for large and pleasant navigable rivers, heaven and earth never agreed better to frame a place for man's habitation....Here are mountaines, hils, plaines, valleyes, rivers, and brookes, all running more pleasantly into a faire bay, compassed but for the mouth, with fruitful and delightsome land."

The bay region at the beginning of the seventeenth century truly was a fruitful and delightsome land. The air was clear, the climate hospitable. The waters and woods were full of fish and game, and the soil was fertile. The bay and its many tributaries provided a network of hundreds of miles of safe, navigable waterways—a great water highway system that allowed easy and convenient access to thousands of acres of land. The English called the vast Chesapeake region Virginia, in honor of Elizabeth, the Virgin Queen. They made their first permanent settlement, Jamestown, on the James River in 1607. In 1632 King Charles I granted the northern parts of Virginia, north of the Potomac River, to Cecil Calvert, second Lord Baltimore. This new grant was named Maryland, and the first Maryland colonists arrived from England aboard two ships, the *Ark* and the *Dove*, in March 1634. More colonists followed, and within thirty years they would push far enough up the Potomac and Patuxent rivers to begin settling the southernmost portions of the land we now call Prince George's County.

*T*his early map of Maryland was published in England in 1671. Like most maps of America of that day, the view is from the east, from Europe. The land that later became Prince George's County lies between the Potomac and Patuxent rivers, by the crowned lion. Piscataway, now in the southern part of the county, is clearly marked. It was then an Indian village. Courtesy of the Library of Congress, Geography and Map Division

14

The first Englishman to see Prince George's County—long before Maryland was ever established—was Captain John Smith of Virginia. On his first voyage of discovery out of Jamestown, in June 1608, he sailed up the Potomac all the way to the falls. He wrote, "Here we found mighty Rocks, growing in some places above the ground as high as the shrubby trees...." Courtesy of the Library of Congress, Prints and Photographs Division

Chapter 2

THE BEGINNINGS OF MARYLAND

Maryland was the dream of George Calvert. A native of Yorkshire, born about 1580, he was educated at Oxford and entered a career of government service, working first as secretary to the British statesman Sir Robert Cecil. Knighted in 1617, Calvert rose to high office. He was a member of Parliament, secretary of state, and member of the privy council. On the side, he was also an investor in colonial enterprises; he was a member of the East India Company, the Virginia Company, and the Council for New England. In 1620 he entered into his first independent colonial venture by buying a large tract of land on the island of Newfoundland, off the Canadian coast. There he established a small farming colony named Avalon, and in 1623 he received a charter from the crown granting him broad powers of government. Avalon, under the charter, was no democracy; Calvert ruled it, from England, like a feudal prince. His ultimate goal was to make his colony return a profit. Avalon was as much a business enterprise as it was an outpost of empire.

Not long after receiving the charter for Avalon, George Calvert's political fortunes fell at home. As secretary of state, he sought to improve relations with England's longtime rival, Spain. But neither the Spanish nor many Englishmen were interested in better relations at the time, and all his efforts were frustrated. As relations between the two nations worsened, his political position deteriorated. When the two countries went to war, the question became not whether, but how long, he could remain in government. Calvert eventually did submit his resignation, but, despite the pressures on him, he did not leave office solely for the obvious political reasons. Rather his personal life had taken a turn that would have required his departure in the best of political times. Long attracted to Catholicism, Calvert decided, in the midst of his political difficulties, to become a Catholic and acknowledge the fact publicly. In a Protestant kingdom, in an age not noted for its religious toleration, this decision alone would have cost George Calvert his power and position. Ever grateful for his years of loyal service, King James accepted Calvert's resignation and raised him to the peerage, naming him Baron of Baltimore, in Ireland. But by then—it was 1625—Calvert's main interests were no longer in England or in Ireland. His dream lay across the Atlantic.

George Calvert was determined to make his struggling colonial venture on Newfoundland a success. He poured a lot of money into the enterprise, but with little result. The colonists complained that the summers were too short and the winters too long and hard to farm successfully on the island, but Calvert suspected mismanagement and fraud. He visited Avalon in 1627 and again in 1628 before he, too, concluded that the harsh climate made it useless to continue there. After spending the winter of 1628-1629 on Newfoundland, he sailed south to investigate the warmer climes of the Chesapeake. On his return to England, he petitioned the crown for a land grant there.

Calvert was dealing with a new king, Charles I. King Charles was reluctant to make another grant, but Calvert was persistent. Finally, despite the vigorous objections of the Virginians (who thought the whole of the Chesapeake should be theirs), the king assented. A charter was prepared, but before final approval could be granted, George Calvert died. Thus, it was his eldest son, Cecil Calvert, who on June 20, 1632, received the charter and became the first proprietor of Maryland.

Cecil Calvert, like his father before him, had many motives for establishing the colony called Maryland. He hoped it would be a profitable enterprise and enrich his family. He hoped to convert the Indians to Christianity. He also shared the desire of Englishmen to extend the dominions of their king. But like George Calvert (in his later years), Cecil Calvert had another motivation: the dream to build a society where English Catholics could worship freely and participate fully in public life. He knew an all-Catholic colony would be impossible—the Catholic population of England was too small to support one—so instead he hoped to found a colony where toleration of religious differences would be the fundamental social precept. Although he wanted to sail to Maryland himself, Cecil Calvert found that he would have to remain in England to defend his charter against the challenges of Virginians, anti-Catholics, and others. So when the first party of Marylanders left England in November 1633, he was not among them.

Cecil Calvert's new domain was not uninhabited. Before the first Marylanders arrived, the Indians were here. The Indians of the Chesapeake region were of Algon-

*G*eorge Calvert, first Lord Baltimore.
Courtesy of the Library of Congress,
Prints and Photographs Division

quian stock. They lived in small villages and camps along the rivers and streams, where they hunted, fished, and raised a variety of crops. The Indians of Southern Maryland—where the first colonists settled—were united in a loose confederation known to the English as the Piscataway Confederacy. Their chief—whom the colonists grandly styled an emperor—lived in a village along Piscataway Creek, now part of Prince George's County. Another important village was on the Anacostia River, near the present site of Saint Elizabeth's Hospital. The Virginians,

as well as English traders, visited the Piscataways many times before the first Marylanders came on the scene, and fought with them on several occasions. About the time the Maryland colonists arrived, the Piscataways were being pressured by a more warlike tribe to the north, the Susquehannocks, who were ranging into their territory and raiding their villages. While somewhat wary of the Marylanders, the Piscataways did not oppose their settlement. They saw in the Marylanders potential allies against the threat from the north.

After a voyage of three and a half months—with stops in Barbados and Virginia—the *Ark* and the *Dove* arrived in the Potomac in March 1634 with the first 140 Marylanders. Most of the colonists were young men, and most were Protestants. A number of gentlemen were on board—the younger sons of the gentry—and they were mostly Catholic. Those who were paying their own way would receive generous grants of land. Those who could not pay their way would have to work as servants for several years before they could own land. It was the promise of land, so hard to come by in England, that brought most of the colonists to Maryland.

Upon arriving in the Potomac, the Marylanders made camp on Saint Clement's Island. Traders advised them to seek the permission of the Piscataway Indians before making a permanent settlement, so Leonard Calvert, the leader of the expedition and brother of the lord proprietor, led the *Dove* up the Potomac to Piscataway Creek to meet the Indian emperor. A Jesuit priest who accompanied the mission, Father Andrew White, wrote of the chief's lukewarm greetings: "He would not bid him goe, neither would he bid him stay, but that he might use his own discretion." Encouraged nonetheless, Calvert returned to Saint Clement's Island, where on March 25, 1634, the colonists proclaimed the establishment of Maryland and celebrated the first mass in English America. Two days later the Marylanders bought from the Indians a village on the mainland that was being abandoned for fear of Susquehannock raids. It was complete with living quarters and cleared fields. The colonists renamed the place Saint Mary's City, and it became Maryland's first settlement.

After the first few difficult years, Maryland's population grew steadily and rapidly. Lord Baltimore's promise of religious toleration, as well as his promise of land, drew the settlers here, a steady stream of Anglicans, Catholics, Presbyterians, Puritans, Quakers, and other dissenters, coming from England, Scotland, Wales, Ireland, and even France. By the 1680s Maryland was the home of 25,000 souls—the most diverse and pluralistic population in North America. The colonists spread far beyond Saint Mary's City. They lived on both shores of the bay and as far north as the Susquehanna River. Every year, more and more land was taken up, and a prosperous agricultural economy developed.

The key to Maryland's success was one crop: tobacco. Maryland's soil and climate were ideal for the growth of tobacco, and the demand for it in England and Europe was great. Very quickly Maryland followed the pattern of her older neighbor, Virginia, and became a tobacco colony. Even though the market for the crop fluctuated, there was always a demand, and even small farmers could support their families by planting the "sotweed." The tobacco was sent back to England for consumption there or reexport to the Continent. In return came coffee, tea, sugar, rum, tools, clothing, and other necessities and luxuries of life. Except for food for the table, Marylanders grew little else but tobacco.

Maryland's tobacco planters did not live together in towns and villages like the settlers of New England. Instead, Maryland's geography—the great water highway system of the Chesapeake—encouraged the dispersion of the population. Wrote Lord Baltimore in 1678: "The people there not affecting to build nere each other, but soe as to have their houses nere the Watters for conveniencye of trade and their Lands on each syde of and behynde their houses by which it happens that in most places there are not fifty houses in the space of Thirty Myles." Port cities and harbor towns were unnecessary and nonexistent in early Maryland. The ships from England called at all the little local landings to collect tobacco and deliver orders of goods from home. The largest town in seventeenth-century Maryland was the provincial capital, Saint Mary's City, and it was a mere village.

As Maryland's tobacco economy developed, so did its political institutions. The early years of the province were often tumultuous ones, full of disputes between the colonists and Lord Baltimore's government, and sometimes among the colonists themselves. More than once there was armed rebellion. But time and time again the rights of the proprietor were confirmed by the crown, even as the rights of the people were broadened. The proprietor appointed the officers of provincial government, but the General Assembly—elected by male freeholders—became a genuine legislative body, even if the proprietor retained the veto power. Closer to the people, the county became the principal unit of local government, and freeholders could be fined for not voting or taking their turn in office when called upon. The principle upon which Maryland was founded—religious toleration—was enshrined in law by the famous Act of Toleration of 1649.

This picture of a prosperous, growing province should not obscure the fact that life could be hard for the individual settler in early Maryland. So many of the luxuries of England were not present here. Housing was crude. The work was hard. Life expectancy was not long, and disease took many before their time. Nevertheless, Maryland grew, by immigration and natural increase. The twin promises of land and freedom made Maryland a beacon for those seeking better lives in a new land.

Maryland was named in honor of the English queen, Henrietta Maria, wife of King Charles I. She was the daughter of King Henry IV of France. Ironically, while George Calvert was secretary of state, he tried to arrange a marriage between Charles and a Spanish princess instead. Courtesy of the Library of Congress, Prints and Photographs Division

Cecil Calvert, the second Lord Baltimore, posed with his grandson (also named Cecil) for this portrait by Gerard Soest. In his hand is a map of Maryland. Courtesy of the Enoch Pratt Free Library, Baltimore

The principal villages of the Indians in the Chesapeake region were usually stockaded. The Indians lived not in tepees, but in small houses covered with bark or rush mats. This drawing actually portrays a Susquehannock village farther north, but Piscataway villages were quite similar. The palms and cattle in the drawing are inaccurate embellishments. From Arnoldus Montanus, *De Nieuwe en Onbekende Weereld* (1671); courtesy of the Library of Congress, Prints and Photographs Division

*M*uch of Indian life in the Chesapeake region revolved around the water. It was similar to this scene from the North Carolina coastal region. From Harriott, *A Briefe and True Report of Virginia* (1590). Courtesy of the Library of Congress, Prints and Photographs Division

*T*hese Indians are making a dugout canoe. From the Indians the colonists learned how to make canoes and quickly adopted them as their own. From Theodor de Bry, *America* (about 1590); courtesy of the Library of Congress, Prints and Photographs Division

Leonard Calvert, younger brother of Cecil Calvert, second Lord Baltimore, was the leader of the first colonial expedition and first governor of Maryland. He was still in his twenties at the time. Courtesy of the Library of Congress, Prints and Photographs Division

A
RELATION
OF
MARYLAND;

Together,

VVith {
A Map of the Countrey,
The Conditions of Plantation,
His Majefties Charter to the
Lord *Baltemore*, tranflated
into Englifh.

Thefe Bookes are to bee had, at Mafter *William Peafley* Efq; his houfe, on the back-fide of *Drury-Lane*, neere the *Cock-pit* Playhoufe; or in his abfence, at Mafter *Iohn Morgans* houfe in high *Holbourne*, over againft the *Dolphin*,
London.

September the 8. *Anno Dom.* 1635.

Lord Baltimore published this pamphlet to attract settlers to his colony. The booklet described the country in glowing terms and included a list of all the provisions a settler would need to start out. Most importantly, though, it outlined the conditions of plantation—the terms for acquiring land in Maryland. Courtesy of the Library of Congress

The first settlers to arrive in Maryland came on two ships, the *Ark* and the *Dove*, in 1634. This ship, a full-scale working replica of a seventeenth-century pinnace, is named the *Maryland Dove* and is very much like the original *Dove*, the smaller of the two original vessels. It is seventy-six feet long, and its draft is six feet. Commissioned in 1978, the *Maryland Dove's* home port is Saint Mary's City. Courtesy of Saint Mary's City Commission

Chapter 3

PRINCE GEORGE'S COUNTY IS SETTLED

The first settlers came to Prince George's County from the south, leaving the older settlements of Southern Maryland behind to move to new lands farther up the Patuxent and Potomac rivers. These pioneers of the 1660s, 1670s, and 1680s came up the rivers by boat and canoe and built simple frame cottages and houses when they arrived. For the first generation, life was not easy. Their plantations were not the elegant country seats of legend; their tobacco fields were little more than tiny clearings in the forest. There were no doctors, churches, clubs, or markets; no newspapers, schools, or theaters; and there was little organized community life. Their landings, on the riverbanks, were their only links to the outside world. There they met the ships from England which came to collect their tobacco and sell them goods from home.

Year by year more settlers came, and in a generation's time the banks of the Patuxent and Potomac were lined with homes, farms, and families. In establishing Prince George's County, the General Assembly followed the practice of "erecting" new counties when new areas of Maryland were settled and populous enough to support a county government. Originally, there had been but one county, Saint Mary's, when all of the colonists lived close to the original settlement. By the time Prince George's County was established, there were already ten other counties in Maryland, five on each shore of the bay.

The counties were the most important units of local government in colonial Maryland, and the county court was the central agency of county government. The county court, in those days, exercised both executive and judicial powers. It levied taxes, built roads and bridges, issued business licenses, granted relief for the poor, and found guardians for orphans, besides hearing civil and criminal cases. Each justice was an important figure in his neighborhood, for, acting alone, he could settle minor disputes, mete out punishment for lesser offenses, and transact certain county business. The sheriff was an important county official, too. His was the single most powerful—and lucrative—position in each county, for he acted as the agent of both the county court and the provincial government. His many and varied duties included making arrests, serving legal papers, keeping the jail, collecting taxes, disbursing government funds, conducting elections, and delivering the orders of the governor and council. The county court, the sheriff, and a number of lesser officeholders constituted the county government, the level of government closest to the people and the one which touched their daily lives. The conduct of county business

was an important responsibility, and counties were not created until the area in question could support a county government and fill its many offices.

Prince George's County was erected on Saint George's Day, April 23, 1696, out of land that had previously been part of Charles and Calvert counties. The population then was probably no more than 2,000. Those settlers who lived along the Potomac River had been part of Charles County, while those along the Patuxent had been part of Calvert. The interior of the county was unsettled, and few had ventured north of the Anacostia River. Prince George's County was still Maryland's frontier, and, compared to the older counties, it was a land of small planters and farmers. A census in 1706, just ten years after the county's founding, revealed that there were 406 households in the county, but only thirty-seven men who owned more than 1,000 acres of land. Because there were few large plantations, there were few African slaves. Indentured servants—men and women from Great Britain who surrendered their freedom for a few years in return for passage to the New World—still satisfied most of the need for additional labor. Slaves would not be brought here in large numbers until the eighteenth century.

In 1696 the white residents of the new Prince George's County shared their county with the Piscataway Indians, most of whom then lived in reserved lands along Piscataway Creek. Once these Indians had lived all over Southern Maryland, but as the region filled with white settlers, they withdrew to the Piscataway-Accokeek area. By the time Prince George's County was created, white settlement had leapfrogged beyond them. They could no longer hunt freely and were expected to observe the white man's property rights. For fifty years they had lived peacefully with the settlers, but by 1696 they decided to move on. Despite the entreaties of the Marylanders, who genuinely wanted them to stay, the Piscataways left the province in 1697. Thus, only one year after the founding of the county, Prince George's Piscataway Indians were gone. After some wandering, they eventually settled in Pennsylvania, where they were absorbed by other tribes.

The Piscataways were not the only Indians the Prince Georgeans had to deal with, however. From time to time Senecas and other Indians came south into Maryland, sometimes to trade, but sometimes to fight. The provincial government established companies of rangers to patrol the frontier and warn settlers of Indian movements. At the time of the founding of Prince George's County, these rangers patrolled the area beyond the Anacostia River, venturing as far north as Sugarloaf Mountain and then moving eastward to meet Baltimore County's rangers. The settlers behind this line—the pioneers of Prince

George's County—undoubtedly were grateful for the protection, and many Prince Georgeans took part in the patrols. Still, from time to time hostile Indians slipped through, and from time to time families along the Anacostia River, Rock Creek, and the upper reaches of the Patuxent were harassed, and sometimes hurt. But there were never any massacres, and as the land beyond Prince George's County was settled, the threat of Indian raids disappeared.

In discussing the founding of Prince George's County it would be misleading not to mention that the original boundaries of the county were not the same as they are today. Actually, the "land beyond Prince George's County" referred to above was actually part of Prince George's County until 1748. The act of the assembly which created Prince George's County assigned all of Maryland west of the Patuxent River and north of Mattawoman and Swanson's creeks (the northern boundaries of Charles County) to Prince George's. Thus, Montgomery, Frederick, Washington, Allegany, and Garrett counties; part of Carroll County; and all of the District of Columbia were once part of Prince George's County. Most of this vast area was uninhabited in 1696; that is why it was attached to Prince George's. There was little settlement beyond the present limits of Prince George's until the 1730s, when Germans from Pennsylvania began settling in the Monocacy valley. When that area became populous enough to support a county government of its own, the assembly erected Frederick County. The assembly decreed that the boundary between Prince George's and Frederick counties would be an imaginary line drawn from the mouth of Rock Creek (on the Potomac River) to Seth Hyatt's plantation on the Patuxent. That line is still Prince George's northern boundary, now dividing Prince George's County from Montgomery County, erected out of the southern part of Frederick in 1776.

There is, in truth, much more to the story of the establishment of Prince George's County than the simple fact of an act of the General Assembly. Prince George's County was born out of revolution, one of the products of a fundamental change in the government and religious order of the province. The revolution was a Protestant rebellion against Charles Calvert, third Lord Baltimore, and his government—a successful, armed (though bloodless) coup d'etat that was recognized and legitimized, after the fact, by the crown in England.

The principal grievance of the Protestants against Lord Baltimore was both a political and religious one.

While the lord proprietor persecuted no Christian, he appointed only Catholics or relatives to provincial offices. Almost all of the lucrative collectorships, judgeships, and other civil positions were filled by Calverts, their kin, or Catholics. Many of the favored circle held more than one office. While Lord Baltimore was quite happy to appoint Protestants to county judgeships and other county offices, they could aspire no higher, save for election to the provincial assembly. Protestants comprised a majority of the population, yet their faith, it seemed, disqualified them from the highest offices in Maryland.

Events in England in the 1680s only heightened the tension in Maryland. King Charles II died in 1685 and was succeeded by his brother, James II. A convert to Catholicism, an autocrat, and a believer in the divine right of kings, James prorogued Parliament, suspended laws that offended him, insulted the Church of England, and filled the highest offices of state with fellow Catholics. Unpopular with almost every element of society, he was driven from England by force of arms in 1688. Parliament proclaimed the succession of his Protestant daughter, Mary, and her husband, William of Orange, but James, in France, vowed to regain the throne.

News of the Glorious Revolution, as it was called, reached Maryland early in 1689. Protestant leaders, as well as the Catholics in provincial government, waited in vain for a message from Lord Baltimore acknowledging the succession of William and Mary. No such message ever came. In July, militant Protestants, known as the Associators, formed an army, marched on Saint Mary's City, and seized the statehouse. Members of the governor's council, representing Lord Baltimore, tried to rally armed resistance, but they could not muster enough popular support. They surrendered on August 1 and handed the government over to the Associators, who immediately recognized William and Mary as sovereigns of Maryland.

Ironically, Lord Baltimore, in England, had indeed recognized William and Mary, but that message never reached Maryland. On hearing of the revolution in his province, he protested to the British government and sought the crown's aid in ousting the rebels. Such aid was not forthcoming. Instead, the crown recognized the government of the Associators and suspended the Calverts' charter rights. The crown then announced that it would assume governmental control of Maryland itself, and proclaimed Maryland a royal province. Henceforth, provincial officials would be appointed by the crown. Catholics would be barred from office, as they were in England. The Calverts were allowed to retain title to their lands and were granted certain tax revenues, but their role in the governance of Maryland came to an end. Maryland began anew as a royal province.

Maryland's first royal governor, Lionel Copley, arrived in the province in April 1692. Immediately the work of reforming Maryland began. Among the acts of assembly that year was the establishment of the Church of England as the state church of Maryland. Before the revolution, there was little organized Anglican activity in Maryland, for few Anglican clergymen had come to the province. As a result of the revolution, however, the Church of England became the province's official tax-supported church. The province was divided into thirty parishes, and the inhabitants of each, regardless of religion, were taxed to maintain a church and minister. There was little resistance to the establishment of the Church of England in Maryland, despite the fact that most Marylanders were not Anglicans. Of the other non-Catholic sects represented in the province, only the Quakers were well organized enough to object. Their protests fell on deaf ears, and establishment went forward.

Another change in the first years of royal government was the redrawing of the political map of Maryland. In 1694 the capital was moved from Saint Mary's City to Annapolis, on the Severn River. The geographical logic of the move was obvious—Saint Mary's was no longer centrally located, while Annapolis was—but there was more to the move than the simple question of geography. Saint Mary's was the city of the Calverts, in a county with a large Catholic population. A revolution had been accomplished, and Maryland was now a royal, Protestant province. What better way to reinforce that fact than by building a new capital, far away from the old?

The new royal government also reorganized the counties in Maryland. The boundaries of the three old Southern Maryland counties—Saint Mary's, Calvert, and Charles—were redrawn, and a new one, Prince George's, was erected in 1696. Whether there were political reasons behind all of this is unclear, but one thing can be said of the new Prince George's County: it was a strong Protestant area. While there were a number of old distinguished Catholic families here—giving the local gentry a disproportionately Catholic flavor—the Catholic element in the total population was actually very small, perhaps as low

as 5 percent if an accounting in 1708 was accurate. Surviving records do not reveal whether these religious considerations were important in the decision to create Prince George's County or not; perhaps it was simply time to carve out a new county on the frontier. But whatever the case, Prince George's County took its place in Maryland's scheme of government and its residents assumed the responsibilities of self-government.

Before concluding the story of Maryland's revolution in government it would be worthwhile to recount the stories of three of the individuals involved in that affair who became leading citizens of Prince George's County at its founding in 1696.

Foremost among the defenders of Lord Baltimore was Henry Darnall I, a merchant and planter who owned land in several counties, but who died and was buried here in Prince George's. Darnall was a Catholic, a cousin of Lord Baltimore's wife. He came to Maryland in the 1670s, was elected to the General Assembly, and was appointed to a number of local and provincial offices. When Lord Baltimore left Maryland in 1684, Darnall was a member of the governor's council and became a member of the board of deputy governors charged with running the provincial government in Baltimore's absence. He supported the unpopular James II, as revealed in a letter he wrote in March 1689 praying for his "happy restoration without bloodshed" (Archives of Maryland). When the Protestant Associators seized the statehouse, it was Darnall who tried unsuccessfully to raise an army to oust them. He signed the articles of surrender for the government and left Maryland in September to join Lord Baltimore in England. He eventually returned as a representative of the Calverts and was appointed to several important posts which administered their lands. He died on June 16, 1711, and was buried at his plantation, Darnall's Delight (also known as The Woodyard), in southern Prince George's County.

Two of the leaders of the Protestant Associators also lived in the new county. Colonel John Addison was a Protestant, an Anglican who came to Maryland in the early 1670s. He came from a mercantile family and worked several years as a merchant and Indian trader in Saint Mary's City before moving far up the Potomac, near the Anacostia River, where he acquired several large tracts of land. He was appointed a justice of Charles County but seems to have held no provincial posts before the revolution. He took a leading role in the rebellion, serving as a member of the Associator's Convention (the assembly elected under their regime) and the Grand Committee of Twenty (their executive committee). With the overthrow of the Calverts, appointments to provincial posts followed:

first as justice of the provincial court, then as a member of the governor's council. When Prince George's County was created he was named commander of the county militia with the rank of colonel. Ironically, a few years after the revolution, Addison's stepdaughter, Barbara Dent, married Henry Darnall's stepson, Colonel Thomas Brooke. Addison died sometime during the winter of 1705-1706.

Ninian Beall was another leader of the Protestant

Queen Anne, wife of Prince George, was still the heir to the throne when Prince George's County was named in her husband's honor. The last of the Stuart monarchs, she was also the last to exercise the royal veto. Of the fourteen children born to Anne and George, only William, the duke of Gloucester, lived much beyond infancy, and he died at age eleven in 1700. Anne died in 1714 and was succeeded by George I, the first of the Hanovers. Courtesy of the Library of Congress, Prints and Photographs Division

rebellion. A native of Scotland, he was a coronet in the army resisting Cromwell when he was captured at the Battle of Dunbar in 1650. He became a political prisoner and was sent first to Barbados, then to Maryland, where he worked as an indentured servant. After obtaining his freedom he amassed vast land holdings and was appointed to a number of local governmental and militia offices, including the office of sheriff of Calvert County. Beall was one of the leaders of the rebel army, and, like Addison, he became a member of the Associators' Convention and the Grand Committee of Twenty. In 1696 he was elected one of Prince George's County's first delegates to the General Assembly. As a militia officer, he led patrols on the frontier whenever there were Indian alarms, and continued to do so well into his seventies. He was a staunch Presbyterian and the owner of much of the land that is now Georgetown in the District of Columbia. In 1717 he died at his home plantation, Bacon Hall, near Upper Marlboro.

On Saint George's Day, April 23, 1696, the newly appointed justices of the Prince George's County court met at a place called Mount Calvert, on the Patuxent River, to take their oaths of office and bring Prince George's County formally into existence. Although everyone called the place Mount Calvert, its official name was Charles Town, and indeed, it was a little town, with a few stores, a church, and an inn or two. As it was the only town within the bounds of the new county, it became the county seat. A courthouse was erected and so was a cage, a pillory, a whipping post, and stocks. For twenty-five years Charles Town served as our county seat, until the General Assembly decided that Upper Marlboro, a newer, bigger, and more convenient town four miles away, should have the honor. On March 28, 1721, the court convened in Charles Town, recessed, and then reconvened a few hours later in Marlboro. Charles Town faded away, and now, more than 250 years later, its name is almost forgotten. One large brick home marks the site. The casual visitor who ventures off Route 382 to explore Mount Calvert Road could hardly be expected to know that at its end, down by the river, there was once a place named Charles Town, and that this was where Prince George's County had its beginning.

One final ironic note must be appended to the story of Maryland's revolution in government. In 1715 old Charles Calvert, third Lord Baltimore, died. His son, Benedict Leonard Calvert, became the fourth Lord Baltimore. Although born a Catholic, he had become an Anglican. With his succession to the title, the crown restored the Calverts' powers of government and once again Maryland became a proprietary province.

THE
DECLARATION
OF THE
REASONS and MOTIVES
For the PRESENT
Appearing in Arms
OF
THEIR MAJESTIES
𝔓𝔯𝔬𝔱𝔢𝔰𝔱𝔞𝔫𝔱 𝔖𝔲𝔟𝔧𝔢𝔠𝔱𝔰
In the PROVINCE of
MARYLAND.

Licens'd, *November* 28th 1689. J. F.

Although the Nature and State of Affairs relating to the Government of this Province, is so well and notoriously known to all Persons any way concerned in the same, as to the People and Inhabitants here, who are more immediately Interested, as might excuse any *Declaration* or *Apology* for this present inevitable *Appearance:* Yet forasmuch as (by the *Plots*, Contrivances, *Insinuations*, *Remonstrances*, and *Subscriptions*, carried on, suggested, extorted, and obtained by the Lord *Baltemore*, his Deputies,
A   'ties,

*T*he Protestant Associators who seized control of the Maryland government in 1689 published their reasons for doing so. Among the revolutionaries were a number of Prince Georgeans. Courtesy of the Library of Congress, Rare Book and Special Collections Division

*C*harles Calvert (1637-1715), third Lord Baltimore, was the object of Maryland's revolution in government in 1689. His father, Cecil Calvert, sent him to Maryland to be its governor in 1661; he lived here until 1684. He became the third Lord Baltimore after his father's death in 1675. Charles Calvert was the only one of the Lords Baltimore to live in Maryland, although his grandson, the fifth Lord, also named Charles Calvert, visited here in 1732-33. Portrait by Sir Godfrey Kneller; courtesy of the Enoch Pratt Free Library, Baltimore

*H*enry Darnall I, Lord Baltimore's principal defender during the tumultuous days of Maryland's revolution in government, lived for many years in Prince George's County before moving, late in life, to Anne Arundel County. His most important estate here was The Woodyard, a lumbering facility as well as a tobacco plantation. Wealthier by far than most Prince Georgeans, at his death he owned more than one hundred slaves and counted among his possessions five wigs, eleven pairs of gloves, and a cloth suit trimmed with gold. Courtesy of the Maryland Historical Society, Baltimore, bequest of Miss Ellen C. Daingerfield

*E*leanor (Hatton) Brooke Darnall was the wife of Colonel Henry Darnall I. Her first husband had been Major Thomas Brooke (1632-1676) of Brookefield. Both of her husbands were wealthy men; Major Thomas Brooke's father, Robert Brooke, brought twenty-eight servants with him when he came to Maryland in 1650. Three of Eleanor Hatton's sons by Major Thomas Brooke became Jesuit priests; another, Colonel Thomas Brooke (1659-1730), became a Protestant, and, as president of the governor's council, served as acting governor of Maryland in 1720. Eleanor Hatton Brooke Darnall died in 1725. Among the provisions of her will was a grant of ten pounds sterling to be distributed to the poor. Courtesy of Maryland Historical Society, Baltimore, bequest of Miss Ellen C. Daingerfield

*J*ohn Addison, one of the leaders of Maryland's Protestant revolution, owned several plantations along the Potomac shore of Prince George's County. The noted British essayist Joseph Addison was his nephew. Portrait attributed to Gustavus Hesselius; courtesy of the Addison Museum of American Art, Phillips Academy, Andover, Massachusetts

*F*ew houses survive from the earliest years of Prince George's County, but this is one of them. This house is known as Mullikin's Delight and is located on Church Road in the central part of the county. The easternmost portion (on the right) was built by James Mullikin I in the 1690s, and the rest was added sometime early in the eighteenth century. The original house measured twenty by twenty feet, but despite its size and simplicity, it was a home of some distinction; its brick foundation alone set it apart from most of its contemporaries and implied a permanence they did not aspire to. When the clapboards were torn off during a 1930s rehabilitation, brick nogging between the studs was revealed. Mullikin's Delight was owned by five successive James Mullikins before it passed out of the family. The house is also important to the Bowie family, for from Mullikin's Delight came Mary Mullikin, daughter of the first James. She married the Scottish immigrant John Bowie in 1707 and became the mother of the Bowies of Prince George's County. Historic American Buildings Survey photograph; courtesy of the Library of Congress, Prints and Photographs Division

*T*his photograph shows the interior of the westernmost section of Mullikin's Delight, built in the early eighteenth century. The fireplace is three feet deep, and the doors and moldings are original. Historic American Buildings Survey photograph; courtesy of the Library of Congress, Prints and Photographs Division

*O*ne of the finest homes in early Prince George's County was old Oxon Hill Manor, a brick house built in 1710 by Colonel Thomas Addison, son of Colonel John Addison, the Associator. The house stood high on a hill above the Potomac River, near the stream the Addisons named Oxon Run. The name Oxon comes from Oxford University, where several members of the family were educated. This sketch appeared in *One Hundred Years Ago, or the Life and Times of the Rev. Walter Dulany Addison, 1769-1848,* by Elizabeth Hesselius Murray (1895). Courtesy of the Library of Congress

*T*he main hall of old Oxon Hill Manor was photographed in the 1890s. This photograph appeared in the book *Examples of Domestic Colonial Architecture in Maryland and Virginia,* by J. M. Corner (1892). The house was destroyed by fire three years later. Reported the *Alexandria Gazette* on February 7, 1895: "The whole eastern heavens were illuminated by the conflagration—the fire raging furiously, the flames leaping high, while a huge volume of smoke settled over the adjoining hills. Numbers of people in this city went to the streets facing the river to look at the fire, which continued to rage for several hours." Courtesy of the Library of Congress

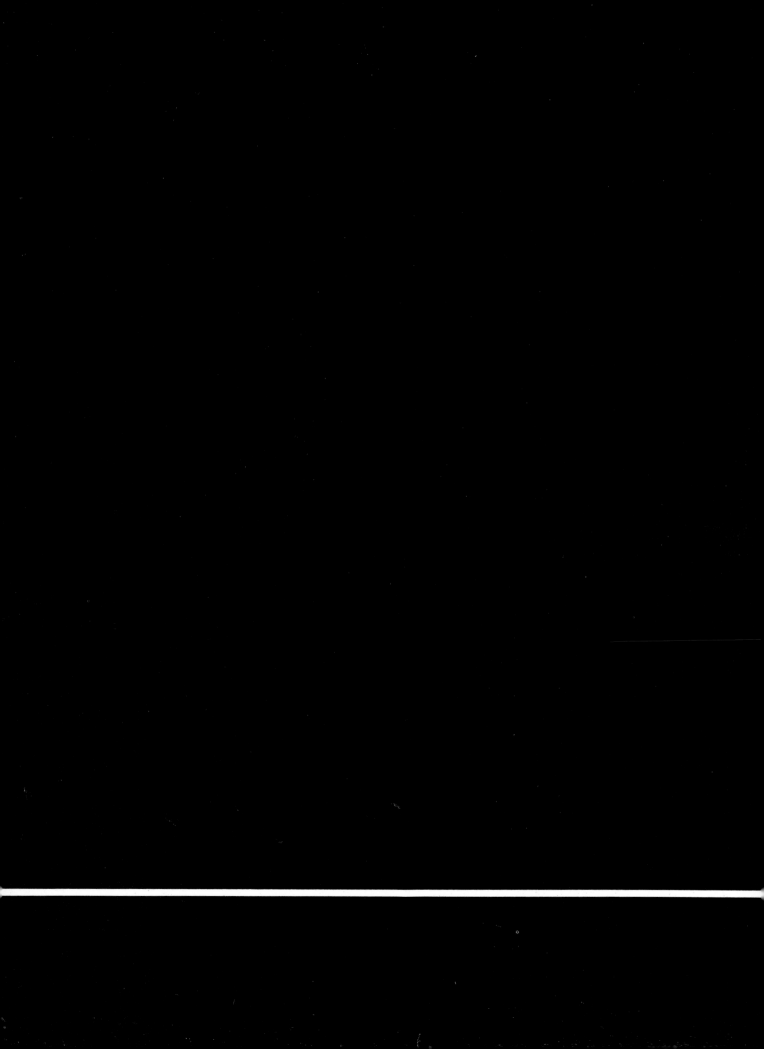

Chapter 4

THE TOBACCO COUNTY

Prince George's County, at its founding in 1696, was still frontier. But as more and more settlers came, and more and more land was taken up, the frontier receded. Within a decade or two the danger of Indian raids from the unknown beyond disappeared. In a generation's time, or perhaps a little longer, Prince George's County became a well-settled land of farms and families, good roads and byways, of doctors, lawyers, storekeepers, and merchants. The southern areas of the county, particularly on the Patuxent side, experienced this change first, but gradually, as the decades of the eighteenth century rolled by, so too did the other sections of the county. By the midpoint of the century not a section of the county was unsettled. The frontier was gone. The pioneers were now the men and women of Western Maryland, beyond the Monocacy, out toward the mountains. Prince George's County had become a populous, well-established agricultural community, where all the amenities of civilized colonial country life could be found.

The foundation upon which the development of Prince George's County rested was the culture of tobacco. Both small farmers and rich planters were tobacco growers. When the tobacco market was good, Prince George's County prospered. When the market was depressed, all Prince Georgeans felt it.

The yearly cycle of tobacco cultivation began in the late winter or early spring with the sowing of the seeds in seedbeds. In June the small plants were transplanted into the fields, into rows of tobacco hills. Every day, all summer long, the tobacco was weeded, hoed, and inspected for worms and insects. When flowers began to appear, the plant tops were broken off to encourage fuller and stronger leaf growth. A few weeks after topping— by September—the plants were four to seven feet high and ready to be harvested. The entire plant was cut and hung in barns to dry. Over the winter, the leaves were stripped off the stalks, tied into hands, and packed into huge casks called hogsheads. The tobacco then was ready to be sold or stored. Tobacco commanded such a leading place in Maryland's colonial economy that it became a medium of exchange. Taxes were assessed, debts paid, and land priced not in pounds sterling but in pounds of tobacco. Maryland could truly be called a tobacco colony, and Prince George's was without a doubt a tobacco county.

It was during the eighteenth century that African slaves were first brought to Prince George's County in large numbers. Most of the settlers came as small farmers and worked in the tobacco fields with their families. But tobacco demanded daily attention, and the most a farmer could tend himself was two or three acres. To increase production beyond this subsistence level—to better himself economically—the farmer needed additional labor. In the seventeenth century, those who could afford extra hands usually took on indentured servants. But that changed in the eighteenth century. As the farmers and planters became more numerous and prosperous, they found that their need for additional labor could no longer be met by the supply of indentured servants, whose numbers were limited and terms of service temporary. So instead of indentured servants they turned to slave labor. By the early eighteenth century approximately a quarter of the households in Prince George's County owned slaves. By the 1750s that figure may have reached half; it was indeed that high by the time of the American Revolution. Slaveholding, then, was not confined to a small upper class. It was widespread in eighteenth-century Prince George's County.

What kind of lives did slaves lead in Prince George's County? Whether they lived on large plantations or small ones, working with other slaves or alone, most were farm laborers. They worked in the tobacco fields in the summer and did other farm chores during the rest of the year. Some, on the largest plantations, were taught trades such as carpentry or cooperage, but their numbers were few. In the early years most slaves, of course, were African-born and spoke a bewildering assortment of African tongues. Wrenched from their homelands, deprived of their freedom, and thrust into an alien environment, they must have had most difficult lives, for they had neither families, friends, nor familiar institutions to comfort them. By the 1750s, however, most slaves here were American-born, born into an evolving and distinct Afro-American culture that helped them cope with slavery and maintain feelings of personal worth and dignity. They grew up with brothers, sisters, and other relatives; as adults they often worked with their families and others they had known since childhood. Their lives were much different from those of the first generation of slaves. Although their destinies were controlled by whites, their personal lives, at least, were lived in a supportive, sympathetic, and familiar Afro-American culture.

Family and kin relationships were particularly important to the slaves, even though they were denied traditional family life. While slave marriages were allowed, even between slaves of different plantations, there were no guarantees that husbands and wives could ever live together or would not be separated. Women thus raised the children. While babies and small children were rarely taken from them, the older ones sometimes were. However, since most slave sales were between relatives or planters who lived near each other, separation did not always mean total loss of contact. Just as particular areas and neighborhoods were identified with certain white families, so too were the slaves of those neighborhoods often interrelated. A community life did develop among slaves, even if it was constrained by the realities of the slave system. Christianity was encouraged, and it was embraced by many.

By the middle of the eighteenth century almost half of this county's population was slave. Some areas, such as the rich plantation neighborhoods near Upper Marlboro, were 60 to 70 percent black. Slavery was a part of life here, and the contributions of the slaves to the building of colonial Prince George's County cannot be overstated.

First the planters and slaves grew tobacco in Prince George's County, and then they built towns. Actually, towns developed slowly in colonial Prince George's. From the earliest settlement, the population was widely scattered and so was economic and social activity. Inns, churches, mills, blacksmiths, and artisans were scattered across the countryside.

Planters and farmers sold their tobacco to merchants or their agents at local landings, and there they received goods shipped from abroad. Sometimes wealthy planters kept stocks of merchandise for sale, but most often shopping was done when the ships came in.

In the late seventeenth and early eighteenth centuries, on several occasions, the Maryland General Assembly directed the establishment of towns. The purpose was to encourage trade and commerce. The assembly further ordered that no tobacco be exported nor goods imported except at these locations. This order proved unenforceable, however, and trading went on in the usual manner, as the planters preferred. The General Assembly's towns did not really develop into trading and social centers until the surrounding neighborhoods were populous and prosperous enough to encourage merchants to open year-round stores there. Only then did local planters find it more convenient to concentrate their buying and selling in these places, and

only then was there enough activity at these sites to warrant calling them true towns.

Charles Town, at Mount Calvert on the Patuxent River, was established by law in the 1680s and was the only town in Prince George's County when it was erected in 1696. Despite its designation as a county seat, Charles Town never became much more than a small village. Several stores and inns operated there, but there was never much of a resident population. Later, when the county court moved to Upper Marlboro, it disappeared.

In 1706 and 1707 the General Assembly directed the establishment of six more towns in Prince George's County: Upper Marlboro, Nottingham, Queen Anne, Mill Town, Piscataway, and Aire (also known as Broad Creek). The first four named were on the Patuxent side of the county, the last two on the Potomac side. Upper Marlboro was the first of these to develop. It lay in the heart of rich tobacco country, in an area that became the most densely settled in colonial Prince George's County. Merchants saw the possibilities of the place and located there; so did innkeepers, tradesmen, and craftsmen. It so eclipsed nearby Charles Town that it was made the county seat in 1721. Among the inhabitants of colonial Upper Marlboro could be found a wigmaker, weaver, tailor, staymaker, coachmaker, and saddler. Concerts, balls, and horse races were among the diversions that entertained the townspeople and brought planters to town; sometimes traveling theater troupes also came through. Slaves could be bought in Upper Marlboro, too. The *Maryland Gazette* for March 14, 1765, advertised "Eleven valuable negroes: three men, three women, three girls, and five children." By mid-century, several hundred people lived in and around the town, many of them Scottish immigrants who built Prince George's County's first Presbyterian church.

Nottingham, Queen Anne, Piscataway, and Broad Creek did not grow as quickly or as large as Upper Marlboro, but they did become thriving little places in themselves, centers for buying, selling, and socializing in their Patuxent and Potomac river neighborhoods. Of the five towns established by the assembly in 1705 and 1706, only Mill Town failed to develop. As the northern sections of the county were settled, towns developed there, too. The first town in the northern section was Bealltown, located on the Northwest Branch near present-day Hyattsville. Bealltown grew up in the 1720s and 1730s, and like the older towns it became the home of merchants, innkeepers, and craftsmen. But Bealltown was located a little too far upstream, and the inhabitants could not keep the stream open for larger vessels. In 1742, the assembly therefore directed the establishment of Bladensburg a mile or so downstream. Bladensburg grew quickly, and soon Bealltown was abandoned. Bladensburg's port, located on the Anacostia River (then called the Eastern Branch), easily accommodated the large vessels Bealltown could not. By the time of the Revolution, Bladensburg was one of the most active tobacco ports in Maryland, exporting more tobacco than any other on the Western Shore. Some early industrial concerns were also built there: a tannery, a shipyard, a ropewalk, and a gunpowder plant. The traffic on two new important roads—the road up to Frederick County and the road north (today's Route One) added to the town's bustle. Bladensburg, in the colonial era, was second only to Upper Marlboro in population and importance, and there were many—particularly in Bladensburg—who wished to see the county seat moved there.

A change in the method of marketing tobacco further encouraged the growth of towns in Prince George's County in the second half of the eighteenth century. In 1747, in response to years of poor prices for Maryland tobacco and numerous complaints from merchants concerning its quality, the General Assembly established a formal system of tobacco inspection and quality control. No longer could planters sell their tobacco directly to tobacco merchants. Instead, they first had to bring it in to public tobacco warehouses for inspection and grading. There, after inspection, the hogsheads could be stored, and the planters would receive certificates stating the quantity deposited. Tobacco marketing thus moved away from all the small local landings and became concentrated at the sites of these warehouses. Of the seven tobacco warehouses initially established in Prince George's County, six were in towns—Upper Marlboro, Bladensburg, Queen Anne, Nottingham, Piscataway, and Broad Creek. The other was at Magruder's Landing, a place on the Patuxent River in the county's southeastern corner. This system of tobacco inspection seemed to work, and the planters themselves sought its renewal in subsequent assembly sessions. The towns benefited, too, for they profited from the increased activity the warehouses brought them.

In concluding the story of Prince George's colonial towns, it is necessary to mention four other towns, two in Prince George's County and two nearby. The first, Hamburgh, was located on land which is now part of the District of Columbia, on the Potomac River near Constitution Avenue. Founded in 1767, it was a German town, the only colonial settlement of non-Britons within the post-1748 bounds of Prince George's County. The other county town, Carrollsburgh, was founded in 1771 and was located at Buzzard's Point, now in southwest Washington, D.C. Neither Hamburgh nor Carrollsburgh grew to much size, however, and they existed more on plat maps and in sales books than they did in reality. Two nearby towns outside of Prince George's County did, however, become important centers of commerce. Alexandria, on the Virginia side of the Potomac, became a leading seaport and the commercial center for all of Northern Virginia. Georgetown, at Rock Creek, was located just below the falls of the Potomac River, and in the 1750s and 1760s it became the center of trade in lower Frederick County. When Montgomery County was erected in 1776, Georgetown was its only port accessible to seagoing ships.

The colonial towns of Prince George's County were important in the county's development, for commercial, social, and cultural opportunities could be found there that were not present in the countryside. But it must be remembered that most inns, churches, mills, blacksmiths, artisans, and even merchants were still out in the country, and that colonial Prince George's County remained very much an agricultural county.

To those acquainted with our history, the phrase "colonial Prince George's County" brings to mind the great homes that are the enduring legacy of that era. They are our pride, testaments to the wealth and grace that once were the hallmarks of Prince George's society. Not everyone in the colonial era lived in such houses, though; indeed, most did not. But in an age much more deferential to wealth and social position than this one, the owners of those homes set the tone of public life, and Prince George's County gained a reputation as a place of fine and gracious living.

How different the Prince George's County of the late colonial era was from that of 1696! The frontier was gone, and with it the unbounded opportunity and social mobility that could be found there. The plantation system of tobacco and slaves brought wealth to many, but it also transformed the frontier into a much less fluid, more stratified society. Families who accumulated wealth in the early years—wealth in the form of land and slaves—passed it on from one generation to the next, giving rise to a hereditary gentry of wealth, power, and social position. It became harder and harder for people of average means to buy the land and labor necessary to raise enough tobacco to become wealthy; indeed, it became more difficult, even with a slave or two, to maintain a moderately comfortable lifestyle. No longer could an indentured servant like Ninian Beall expect to become a man of wealth and power. By the end of the colonial era, new immigrants from Europe, ambitious men and women of lesser means, and even the younger sons of the local gentry were leaving Prince George's County behind for opportunity elsewhere. By 1790 the free population of Prince George's County reached 10,000 and stopped growing. It would not grow again as long as the plantation system survived.

The Prince George's County of the late colonial era was much different from the frontier county of 1696 in another important respect, too: the matter of religion. The Church of England was newly established as the state church of Maryland when Prince George's County was erected, and most residents were still unchurched, with little contact with organized religion. But gradually, over the years, that unchurched society became an Anglican one. Small Catholic and Presbyterian minorities clung to their faiths, but through the course of the eighteenth century most Prince Georgeans came to think of themselves as Anglicans, at least at baptism, wedding, and burying times. Methodism was introduced here in the 1770s and quickly attracted many adherents, but religious diversification went no further. Save for a few scattered individuals, Prince Georgeans at the close of the century were either Anglican, Methodist, Catholic, or Presbyterian.

Prince Georgeans, like their counterparts elsewhere in the thirteen colonies, participated in the great events of the Revolution. They formed local committees of correspondence and safety, organized boycotts of British goods, and went off to war to fight for the cause of independence. A few—notably members of the Anglican clergy and the Calvert family—sat out the conflict, but active Loyalists were hard to find. British ships occasionally entered the Potomac and Patuxent rivers, harassing the planters on their banks, but the enemy never launched a serious invasion. The greatest excitement came in 1781 when British ships put some men

ashore at the mouth of Piscataway Creek to forage for food. Several parties came ashore over the course of several days, each time encountering resistance from the local militia. The ships finally departed.

Since Maryland was not the scene of any major fighting during the Revolution, Prince George's Revolutionary War heroes won their glory elsewhere: Rezin Beall at Harlem Heights, Luke Marbury at Germantown; and Edward Duvall at the siege of Ninety-Six, South Carolina, to name only three. Others contributed to the cause of independence through statecraft. Prior to the war, William Murdock, of Padsworth Farm (near Queen Anne), represented Maryland at the Stamp Act Congress of 1765. John Rogers of Upper Marlboro sat in Congress on the day the Declaration of Independence was approved—and voted for its adoption—but failed to return to Philadelphia to add his signature to the document once it was engrossed. Thus Prince George's County cannot claim to be the home of a Signer, and the name of John Rogers, remembered locally, is forgotten in other parts of the nation he voted into being.

Perhaps the most noteworthy contribution Prince George's County made to the Revolutionary cause came not in battle or in statecraft, but in the less dramatic field of military supply. Stephen West—importer, exporter, and owner of several stores in the county—turned his plantation, The Woodyard (once a Darnall property) into a great gun manufactory. His slaves built and repaired muskets for Maryland troops, and they made powder, blankets, stockings, and woolen cloth as well. Another county merchant, Christopher Lowndes, supplied the infant Maryland navy with cordage from his ropewalk near Bladensburg. The economic sacrifices of the families at home were great during the war, but at its conclusion, with peace and nationhood secured, Prince Georgeans returned to their lives of old, whatever their places were in the tobacco society of two hundred years ago.

During the seventeenth and early eighteenth centuries, most Prince Georgeans lived in small frame houses like this one. They had, at the most, two or three rooms, and the chimneys were made of wattle and daub. In her book *Tobacco Colony* (1982), historian Gloria Main calls them "throwaway houses," for they were hastily (and inexpensively) built of green wood and then readily abandoned when it was time to move on to new fields elsewhere on the plantation. Visitors to early Maryland often complained of the number and unsightliness of abandoned houses. None of these early structures survives in Prince George's County today, although one like them has been built at Patuxent River Park near Croom. This replica is at Saint Mary's City. Brick chimneys, incidentally, did not replace the wattle-and-daub ones until the eighteenth century, except on finer homes.
Courtesy of Saint Mary's City Commission

This old home, known as Mount Calvert, is all that stands on the site of Charles Town, the first county seat of Prince George's County. Tradition holds that this house stood in Charles Town, but historical research and architectural evidence suggest that it was probably built in the late eighteenth century or in the very early years of the nineteenth century, long after Charles Town had faded away. Historic American Buildings Survey photograph; courtesy of the Library of Congress, Prints and Photographs Division

A MAP of the most INHABITED part of VIRGINIA containing the whole PROVINCE of MARYLAND with Part of PENSILVANIA, NEW JERSEY AND NORTH CAROLINA Drawn by Joshua Fry & Peter Jefferson in 1751.

To the Right Honourable, George Dunk Earl of Halifax First Lord Commissioner and to the Rest of the Right Honourable and Honourable Commissioners for TRADE and PLANTATI...

This Map is most humbly Inscribed to their Lordships.

This scene, taken from an eighteenth-century map, incorporates three of the most important elements in the colonial economy of Prince George's County—tobacco, ships, and slaves. Here at the port, the planters brought their tobacco for inspection, grading, and storage until shipment to England. This scene must have been played out many times at the two busiest ports in Prince George's County, Upper Marlboro and Bladensburg, both of which had large tobacco warehouses. Upper Marlboro's port was located at the end of Water Street on the Western Branch of the Patuxent River. Bladensburg's was on the Anacostia, near Peace Cross. Silt from generations of farming made the Western Branch unnavigable, even in the late eighteenth century, while the last commercial vessel of any size to leave Bladensburg was the sailing ship *Rover*, loaded with sixty hogsheads of tobacco in 1843. Courtesy of the Library of Congress, Geography and Map Division

43

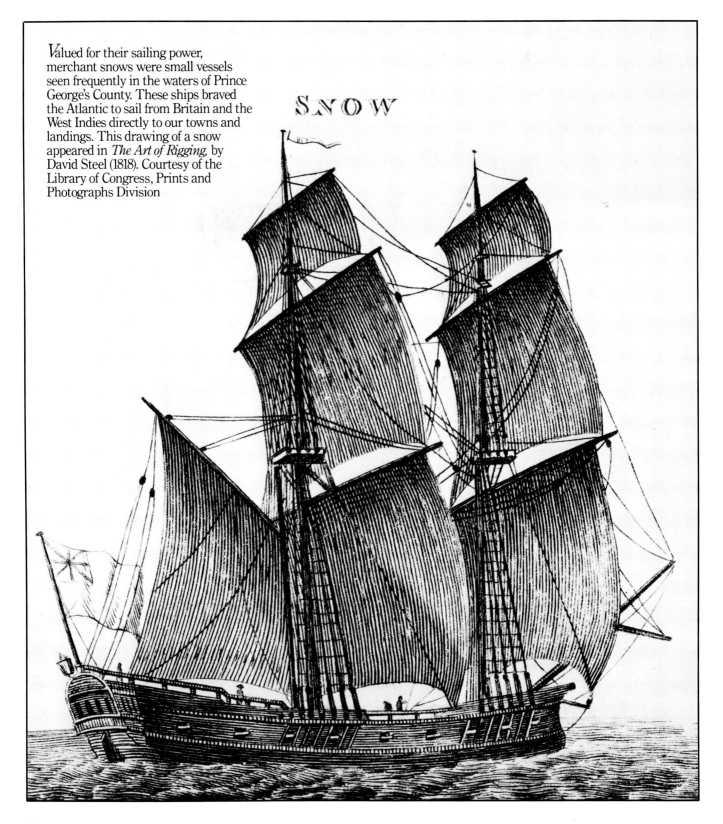

*V*alued for their sailing power, merchant snows were small vessels seen frequently in the waters of Prince George's County. These ships braved the Atlantic to sail from Britain and the West Indies directly to our towns and landings. This drawing of a snow appeared in *The Art of Rigging*, by David Steel (1818). Courtesy of the Library of Congress, Prints and Photographs Division

SNOW

The parts of the tobacco plant are shown in drawings from *An Historical and Practical Essay on the Culture and Commerce of Tobacco,* by William Tatham, published in 1800. It was the leaf, of course, that brought wealth to Marylanders. Courtesy of the Library of Congress, Prints and Photographs Division

These scenes show tobacco being conveyed to market, from Tatham. In Prince George's County the ox was used as much, if not more, than the horse. Courtesy of the Library of Congress, Prints and Photographs Division

Across the countryside, wealthy planters built homes of distinction. Melwood Park is a fine country home outside of Upper Marlboro. The house was built about 1729 by William Digges, the son of Colonel William Digges of Warburton Manor. George Washington dined here several times with his friend, Ignatius Digges, the son of the builder. During the War of 1812, British officers invited themselves in for dinner and made this their headquarters one night on their march to Washington. Courtesy of the Enoch Pratt Free Library, Baltimore

The surveying of plantations was an important proprietary function during the colonial era. The limits of each plantation were defined by metes and bounds; no grid pattern of townships and sections was ever superimposed on the land of Prince George's County. This is a 1759 plat of the Mount Pleasant plantation on the Patuxent River. It was actually more regularly-shaped than most, but its legal boundaries were still marked by stones, hickory stumps, and cherry trees. Mount Pleasant came into the Waring family during the eighteenth century. Waring descendants still own the old plantation house and surrounding acreage; the modern community of Marlboro Meadows was built on much of the rest. Courtesy of the Hall of Records, Annapolis

Upper Marlboro, the county seat, was Prince George's County's first important town. The town was named in honor of John Churchill, duke of Marlborough, victor over the French at Blenheim in 1704. Another Maryland town, farther down the Patuxent River in Calvert County, was also named for the duke; it became Lower Marlboro.

This house, the oldest in Upper Marlboro, was moved to Calvert County in 1971. In 1704 Edward Digges built it as a tavern, and it stood on Water Street on the way to the port. The first tavernkeeper was John Decora. Wrote James C. Wilfong, Jr.: "There is a pleasing balance and proportion of dormer windows to roofline; if you have a liking for early Maryland, you will have a tremendous liking for this property." In recent years it was known as the Wilson House, for the last Upper Marlboro family to own it. Historic American Buildings Survey photograph; courtesy of the Library of Congress, Prints and Photographs Division

*H*armony Hall, one of the prettiest of Prince George's County's colonial homes, is near Broad Creek, off of Livingston Road. The traditional date of construction is 1723. In 1793 it was rented by Walter Dulany Addison and his brother John for themselves and their new brides; their happy year there prompted the name. This is the river front. Harmony Hall is now owned by the National Park Service. Historic American Buildings Survey photograph; courtesy of the Library of Congress, Prints and Photographs Division

The symbol of old Upper Marlboro, the Marlborough House, was built in the first decade of the eighteenth century as a residence for Dr. Patrick Hepburn, one of the early justices of the Prince George's County court. The Marlborough House was one of colonial Upper Marlboro's finest homes; its mantles were renowned, and the brick arch above the door was much admired. Through its long history it saw both residential and commercial uses, serving as a bank, a hotel, a tavern, and a store as well as a home. The wing on the left was added in 1858 when the building became the Marlborough House hotel. The entire structure was destroyed in 1957.

The image of the Marlborough House is engraved in silver on the coffee waiter of the old U.S.S. *Maryland* (1906), on display in the statehouse in Annapolis. The stone footings of the Marlborough House, said to be more than three feet wide, still rest under the pavement of the parking lot that took its place. The Marlborough House stood perpendicular to Main Street, which is on the right in this picture. Historic American Buildings Survey photograph; courtesy of the Library of Congress, Prints and Photographs Division

High on a hill on the west side of Upper Marlboro is Kingston, believed to have been built about 1730 by the merchant David Craufurd. The house rests on a brick basement, and the chimneys are freestanding. Kingston remained in the Craufurd family until 1859 when it was bought by Dr. Frederick Sasscer. Among its subsequent residents was Judge T. Van Clagett, Dr. Sasscer's son-in-law, who for more than twenty-five years was a member of Upper Marlboro's board of commissioners. Historic American Buildings Survey photograph; courtesy of the Library of Congress, Prints and Photographs Division

Dunblane was a modest home, but it was one of Prince George's County's most venerable landmarks because of its association with the earliest generations of the Magruder family. Dunblane was built in 1723 by John Magruder, grandson of Alexander Magruder, the Scottish immigrant. It stood near Forestville until a gas explosion destroyed it on Good Friday 1969. Three walls were of brick, the fourth of logs. At its destruction, Dunblane was the oldest Magruder home in Maryland. The frame addition attached to the left rear of the main house was added many years after the original was built. Historic American Buildings Survey photograph; courtesy of the Library of Congress, Prints and Photographs Division

This is a side view of Dunblane, from the northwest. Not one of the windows was the same size as another. Historic American Buildings Survey photograph; courtesy of the Library of Congress, Prints and Photographs Division

Six churches in Prince George's County have survived from colonial times, five of them Episcopalian and one of them Catholic. They are all country churches, for most of our colonial churches were found in the countryside, not in the towns. Only the Presbyterians seemed to favor town sites, but none of their colonial churches (in Upper Marlboro or Bladensburg) are still on the scene.

The oldest church in Prince George's County is Saint Paul's Episcopal at Baden. Saint Paul's was built between 1733 and 1735 to replace an older and deteriorating Anglican structure in Charles Town, once the county seat. The parish which it serves was one of the thirty original parishes formed in Maryland when the Church of England was established here in 1692. Originally rectangular in form, Saint Paul's has been enlarged and is now in the shape of a Latin cross. The sundial over the door—unique in Prince George's County church architecture—was purchased in England in 1751. The setting of Saint Paul's is still a rural one, in the old southeastern section of the county. Historic American Buildings Survey photograph; courtesy of the Library of Congress, Prints and Photographs Division

The rector of Saint Paul's parish for nearly fifty years was the Reverend John Eversfield. A native of Kent, England, he was educated at Oxford and came to Maryland as a young priest in 1728. Saint Paul's was the only appointment he ever accepted; he ministered first at the old church in Charles Town and then supervised the building of the new church several miles away. He served as rector of the parish until 1776. In 1730 he married one of his parishioners, Miss Eleanor Clagett, and they had several children.

Mr. Eversfield kept a large parchment volume of more than 700 pages, containing deeds, surveys, genealogies, correspondence, notes, and an autobiography. A microfilm copy is kept at the Hall of Records in Annapolis. Mr. Eversfield was also a teacher, maintaining a school until his death in 1780. Portrait by an unknown artist; courtesy of the Maryland Historical Society, Baltimore, bequest of Mrs. Virginia Bowie Schoenfeld

*T*homas John Claggett (1743-1816) was the first Episcopal bishop consecrated in this country. His consecration as bishop of Maryland marked the beginning of a new era in the history of the Protestant Episcopal Church here, for it signalled the transformation of the church into a truly American one, no longer tied to the Church of England.

Claggett was born near Nottingham, the son of a cleric. He received his early education from his uncle, the Reverend John Eversfield, and completed his schooling at the Lower Marlboro Academy (in Calvert County) and at Princeton, where he received a master's degree. He served first in Calvert County before becoming rector of Saint Paul's parish in 1780. He relinquished the post in 1786, but assumed it again in 1792, holding the rectorship even while bishop of Maryland. Bishop Claggett was a big man, about six feet four inches tall. His remains and those of his wife rested in the family burying ground at his home plantation, Croom, until they were reinterred at the Washington Cathedral in 1898. Courtesy of the Library of Congress, Prints and Photographs Division

*S*aint Thomas Church at Croom was built in the early 1740s as a chapel for Saint Paul's parish, for the convenience of those parishioners living in the northern part of the parish. The first services were held here in 1745. This was the home church of Thomas John Claggett, a native of Prince George's County who became the first bishop of Maryland in 1792. The bell tower was added in his honor in 1888. James H. Shreve photo; courtesy of Saint Thomas Episcopal Church, Croom

The great Methodist evangelist George Whitefield visited Prince George's County in 1739, preaching in Upper Marlboro while on a tour of the colonies. The Methodists were originally evangelical Anglicans; they did not formally establish a separate church in this country until 1784.

Other Methodist evangelists followed Whitefield here. In his diary, Francis Asbury recorded nine visits to the home of Shadrick and Sarah Turner between the years 1777 and 1801. The Turner farm was located along Edmonston Road, near the Greenbelt Cemetery. Asbury is also known to have visited the forerunners of Immanuel Church in Horsehead, and Bell's Church in Camp Springs. In 1791, Ezekiel Cooper of Virginia "went over the Potomac and preached in Oxenhill in a small preaching house which has been built by a number of religious black people." That early black Methodist congregation is now organized as Saint Paul's United Methodist Church on Saint Barnabas Road. It is probably the oldest black congregation in the county. Courtesy of the Library of Congress, Prints and Photographs Division

Sacred Heart Church at Whitemarsh, in Bowie, is one of the few Catholic church buildings in Maryland dating from colonial times. After the Protestant Revolution of 1689, Catholics were forbidden to worship publicly, and the church was not allowed to own land. In 1728 James Carroll willed 2,000 acres to a Jesuit priest, and on that land a small stone chapel (on the right) was built about 1741. The chapel and the land were passed down from priest to priest, as individuals, until the prohibition against church ownership was lifted after the American Revolution. The larger structure on the left was built sometime later, before the 1820s. Both sections were heavily damaged by fire in 1853, but they were rebuilt in 1856. The bridge that crosses the Patuxent River near Whitemarsh—now carrying Route 3—has long been known as Priests' Bridge, in recognition of the early Jesuit presence in the area. Historic American Buildings Survey photograph; courtesy of the Library of Congress, Prints and Photographs Division

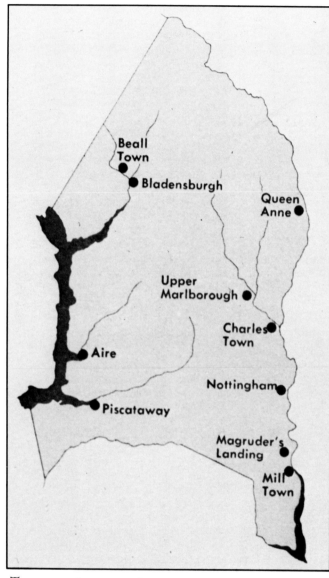

*T*hese were the towns of Prince George's County in 1748. Charles Town and Beall Town were already fading; Mill Town never really developed. From *Prince George's Heritage,* by Louise Joyner Hienton (1972). Courtesy of Dr. Truman E. Hienton

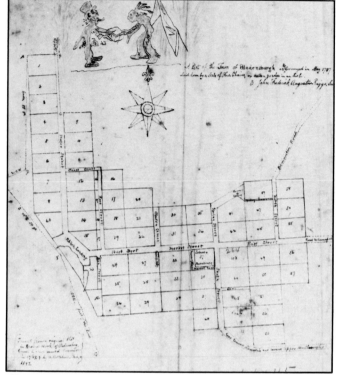

*B*ladensburg, on the Anacostia River, was an important tobacco port during the colonial era. This plat shows the original town plan of 1742 as resurveyed in 1787. Although much has changed in Bladensburg, the basic plan survives: Water Street is now called Baltimore Avenue (Alternate Route One), and West, Market, and East streets have become Annapolis Road (Route 450). Before the river silted in, oceangoing vessels took on tobacco at the public landing. Today that is the site of Peace Cross. Courtesy of the Prince George's County Historical Society

On a rise above the Anacostia River in Bladensburg is Bostwick, built in 1746 by Christopher Lowndes, the leading merchant in colonial Bladensburg. Lowndes came to Maryland in the 1730s to work for Henry and Edward Trafford, merchants of Liverpool, but soon went into business for himself.

Bostwick attests to his success. His store was perhaps the best stocked in Prince George's County; his advertisements in the *Maryland Gazette* promised window glass, writing paper, sheep shears, rat traps, dutch ovens, pewter plates, warming pans, shoe buckles, kid gloves, tomahawks, nutmeg, cloves, Irish linen, white jeans, women's bonnets, silk handkerchiefs, felt hats, and scores of other items. Besides his mercantile concern, Lowndes operated a shipyard and ropewalk near Bladensburg, and was an importer of slaves and indentured servants. He served as a justice of the county court and was a warm supporter of the Revolution. Christopher Lowndes died in 1785 and is buried in the churchyard of Addison's Chapel. Historic American Buildings Survey photograph; courtesy of the Library of Congress, Prints and Photographs Division

This buttress supports the south gable wall of Bostwick. Within are two cells in which were confined unruly slaves. Historic American Buildings Survey photograph; courtesy of the Library of Congress, Prints and Photographs Division

*C*hristopher Lowndes married well. This is his wife, Elizabeth Tasker (1726-1789), daughter of Benjamin Tasker, Esquire, member of the governor's council. At the time of their marriage, the *Maryland Gazette* pronounced her "an agreeable young lady with a good fortune." Elizabeth Tasker's sisters also married distinguished gentlemen: Anne married Governor Samuel Ogle, and Frances married Robert Carter of Virginia. Portrait by John Wollaston, about 1754; courtesy of the Maryland Historical Society, Baltimore, the Blanche Darnall Smith Ferguson Purchase Fund

*T*his little stone house in Bladensburg was built by Christopher Lowndes in 1760. Located on the edge of the market square, near the tobacco warehouse, it probably served a commercial purpose during the colonial era; today it is known as the Market Master's House. Tradition says it was built of ship ballast. An addition was made early in this century, and it is now a residence. This photograph was taken about 1913 by J. Harry Shannon (the "Rambler"), columnist for the old *Washington Star.* Courtesy of the Columbia Historical Society

*T*obacco was not the only crop raised in Prince George's County; grains were also important. Grist mills could be found across the countryside, and this one stood just outside of Bladensburg, in what is now Cottage City. Known as the Carleton Mill or Penn's Mill, it was built in the eighteenth century and functioned until late in the nineteenth. The northern part of Prince George's County was good grain country—better for grain than for tobacco—and this mill was just one of several in the upper Anacostia region. The Carleton Mill stood in ruins until it was finally demolished during the Anacostia flood control project of the 1950s. Two of its millstones survive as part of the sidewalk in the 3700 block of Forty-second Avenue, Cottage City. Courtesy of the Prince George's County Historical Society

*N*ow located at Broad Creek, this home once stood in Piscataway, on the lot next to the Hardy Tavern. It was built around 1750, but its builder is unknown; it came into the possession of Thomas Clagett in 1779. The dormers are unusually decorated. Only the south chimneys are connected by a pent; the northern ones are not. Piscataway House, as it is now known, was in danger of destruction in the 1940s. Charles Collins, then owner of Harmony Hall, dismantled it and moved it to Broad Creek. Courtesy of the Maryland-National Capital Park and Planning Commission, History Division

Samuel Ogle, an Englishman, was appointed governor of Maryland three times. He held office from 1731 to 1732, from 1733 to 1742, and from 1747 until his death in 1752. His first love was horse racing; he imported several fine horses, notably the stallion Spark and the mare Queen Mab, both from the royal stables. His reputation as a breeder of fine horses was widespread, and the Belair estate today is recognized as the cradle of American thoroughbred racing. Ogle was married to Anne Tasker, daughter of Benjamin Tasker, Esquire. Portrait copy by C. Gregory Stapko, 1971; courtesy of the Maryland Commission on Artistic Property

After the death of Governor Samuel Ogle, his widow lived at Belair with her children for several years before turning the management of the plantation over to Colonel Benjamin Tasker, her brother. Colonel Tasker made many improvements to the Belair estate, fencing in a deer park, planting pear trees, building a mill, clearing meadowlands, and creating avenues of locust and poplar leading to the house. Like his brother-in-law, he was a fancier and breeder of fine horses, and he imported the famous mare Selima, another product of the royal stables. Colonel Tasker, like his father, Benjamin Tasker, Esquire, served as a member of the governor's council and held other important provincial posts. He died unmarried in 1760. Portrait by John Wollaston, about 1754. Courtesy of the city of Bowie

*B*elair, on Tulip Grove Drive in the city of Bowie, was built in the 1740s by Benjamin Tasker, Esquire, for his son-in-law, Governor Samuel Ogle. The mansion remained in the Ogle family until 1871, and changed hands several times before it was acquired by James T. Woodward of New York in 1898. The Woodwards added the wings and hyphens and held the property — still a huge estate — until the 1950s, when the Levitt Corporation bought it to build the housing development, "Belair at Bowie." During the 1960s and 1970s it served as Bowie's city hall. Historic American Buildings Survey photograph; courtesy of the Library of Congress, Prints and Photographs Division

*B*enjamin Ogle (1749-1809) was the son of Governor Samuel Ogle. Only three years old when his father died, he was educated in England, but returned to Maryland to claim the Belair estate when he turned twenty-one. His mother wanted to sell the property, and he had to sue to gain possession of it. Like his father, he became governor of Maryland, serving from 1798 to 1801, but governor of a free state, not a province. The home of the two governors, and built by a third (Benjamin Tasker, Esquire, was briefly acting governor), Belair is known as the Home of the Governors. Courtesy of H. Gwynne Tayloe

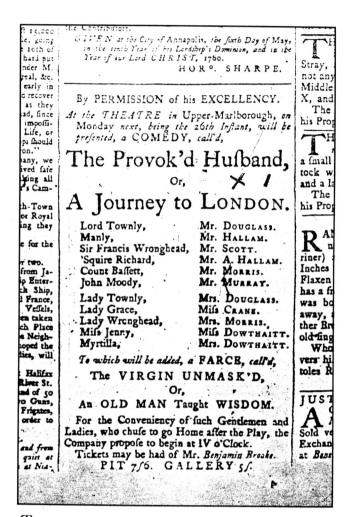

The first scientist in Prince George's County was Dr. Richard Brooke (1716-1783), a physician and planter. He was one of the Brookes of Brookefield, a grandson of Colonel Thomas Brooke and great-grandson of Major Thomas and Eleanor Hatton Brooke. His work on smallpox inoculation was reported in the *Philosophical Transactions of the Royal Society of London,* and so were his meteorological observations, the first known instrumental observations of air temperature and wind direction in Maryland. Dr. Brooke was a patriot as well as a scientist. He served on several local committees during the Revolution and was elected to the Maryland Provincial Convention. Courtesy of the Library of Congress, Rare Books and Special Collections Division

The *Maryland Gazette* of May 22, 1760, advertised a play, The Provok'd Husband, to be presented in Upper Marlboro. The first opera in America known to have been performed with an orchestra was also presented in Upper Marlboro, in 1752; it was the *Beggar's Opera,* by John Gay. Courtesy of the Library of Congress

*C*hrist Episcopal Church in Accokeek was built in 1748 to replace one which the vestry complained had "gone to decay." Originally a chapel of King George's parish (Saint John's Church), it became a parish church in its own right in 1823. Christ Church was gutted by fire on December 23, 1856, leaving only the walls standing. It was rebuilt within six months, incorporating a number of stylistic elements of that later period. Some later renovations were made in 1969. The bell tower has been altered since this photograph was made in the 1930s, and an apse was recently built on the opposite end. Historic American Buildings Survey photograph; courtesy of the Library of Congress, Prints and Photographs Division

*T*he oldest gravestone in the Bladensburg cemetery is that of William Mauduit, who died in 1749. He was one of the original Bladensburg town commissioners (appointed 1742) and was sheriff of Prince George's County from 1746 to 1748. He came from a prominent English mercantile family whose careers are traced in the *Dictionary of National Biography*. Though Mauduit was English, many of his fellow settlers on the upper Eastern Branch (Anacostia River) were Scots. They built a Presbyterian church just south of Bladensburg on land donated for that purpose by Archibald Edmonston in 1725. The church building is long gone, but the burying ground remains. It is now known as Evergreen Cemetery. Hyattsville Presbyterian Church traces its origin to the original Bladensburg congregation. Photo by the author

*M*ount Airy, located in Rosaryville State Park, is the only house left in Maryland known to have been a Calvert home during the colonial era. It was built by Benedict Calvert, son of Charles, fifth Lord Baltimore, about 1760, and was passed down from one generation of the family to the next.

In 1903 the last Calvert owner, Miss Eleanora Calvert, died at Mount Airy in a tragic fall at age eighty-one. The house was acquired by Matilda R. Duvall, who renamed the place the Dower House. Gutted by fire in 1931, the house was rebuilt (and the original name restored) by the publisher of the old *Washington Times-Herald,* Eleanor "Cissy" Patterson. It is now owned by the state. Historic American Buildings Survey photograph; courtesy of the Library of Congress, Prints and Photographs Division

*T*his is another view of Mount Airy. Architectural investigations suggest that some seventeenth-century elements may be incorporated into the small wing on the left (gable end visible). Indeed, there is a tradition that part of the house was built as early as 1660 by the Calverts as a hunting lodge. If there was a seventeenth-century hunting lodge on this site, it may be within that wing. Historic American Buildings Survey photograph; courtesy of the Library of Congress, Prints and Photographs Division

*B*enedict Calvert (1724-1788) was the first Calvert to make Mount Airy his permanent home. The natural son of the fifth Lord Baltimore, he came to Maryland at a young age. He held several important posts in the provincial government. Portrait by John Wollaston, 1754; courtesy of the Baltimore Museum of Art, gift of Alfred R. and Henry G. Riggs

*E*lizabeth Calvert (1730-1798) was the wife and cousin of Benedict Calvert. Her father was Governor Charles Calvert (1688-1733). She and Benedict were married in 1748. Portrait by John Wollaston, 1754; courtesy of the Baltimore Museum of Art, gift of Alfred R. and Henry G. Riggs

These were three of the Calvert children of Mount Airy: Charles (1756-1777), Eleanor (1754-1811), and Rebecca (1749-176?). In February of 1774, Eleanor married John Parke Custis, George Washington's stepson, at Mount Airy. Washington had delayed the wedding two years, thinking his stepson too young for marriage, but finally yielded, "contrary to my judgment, and much against my wishes." Nevertheless, he and Benedict Calvert became friends, and he visited Mount Airy a number of times. The portraits of Charles and Eleanor were painted by John Hesselius in 1761. The portrait of Rebecca was painted by John Wollaston in 1754. Courtesy of the Baltimore Museum of Art, gifts of Alfred R. and Henry G. Riggs

*O*n Woodyard Road, not far from Clinton, stands His Lordship's Kindness, a National Register Landmark. Also known as Poplar Hill, His Lordship's Kindness is an elegant and carefully detailed Georgian country home. The decorative work inside the house is every bit as fine as that on the outside. The mansion dates from the mid-to late-eighteenth century and was built by the Darnall family. Some of the ancient vines of ivy that cover the house are as thick as a man's forearm. Historic American Buildings Survey photograph; courtesy of the Library of Congress, Prints and Photographs Division

This picture shows the hall and stair in His Lordship's Kindness. Historic American Buildings Survey photograph; courtesy of the Library of Congress, Prints and Photographs Division

The first mistress of His Lordship's Kindness was Anne Talbot Darnall, wife of Henry Darnall III, whom she married in 1735. Tradition holds that Anne's uncle, the Earl of Shrewsbury, built the mansion as a wedding present for the young couple, and that they named it His Lordship's Kindness in his honor. Unfortunately, the hard facts seem to contradict this charming old story, for Henry Darnall's grandfather, Henry Darnall I, named the land His Lordship's Kindness when he acquired it in 1703. Furthermore, architectural historians now dispute the traditional building date of 1735, claiming that the home's fine details and features place it later in the century. Whatever the case, the house was inherited by Anne's son, Robert Darnall, at her death in 1788, and he, in turn, devised it to his sister's son, Dr. Robert Sewall, in 1801. It remained in the hands of the Sewalls and their Daingerfield descendants until 1929. His Lordship's Kindness has had several owners since, one of whom was Ambassador David K. E. Bruce. Still privately owned, the house is the center of a working farm. Courtesy of Maryland Historical Society, Baltimore, bequest of Miss Ellen C. Daingerfield

66

*S*aint Barnabas Church at Leeland is the parish church for Queen Anne parish, formed in 1704. A brick church was built for the parish in 1710; this is its replacement, built in 1774. The church was restored in 1974, at which time the nineteenth-century stained-glass windows were replaced by clear windows of the colonial style. Queen Anne parish was one of the richest tobacco-producing regions in colonial Maryland; its rectorship was one of the choicest assignments the Anglican Church could offer in the province. Historic American Buildings Survey photograph; courtesy of the Library of Congress, Prints and Photographs Division

The most controversial rector to serve Queen Anne parish was the Reverend Jonathan Boucher, who came to Saint Barnabas in 1771. Boucher was an Englishman and an ardent Tory. More than once he clashed with his parishioners on political matters, and for months he preached with a pair of loaded pistols beside him. A crowd of 200 men once confronted him in the new church. With a pistol in one hand he seized their leader — Osborn Sprigg of Northampton — and together they marched to Boucher's horse. Boucher was allowed to leave without harm. He returned to England with his wife, Eleanor Addison of Oxon Hill, in 1775. Courtesy of the Library of Congress, Prints and Photographs Division

Boucher was a teacher as well as a cleric, and at his home, Castle Magruder, he operated a school for boys. Now known as Mount Lubentia, the house still stands in Largo, not far from the community college. Castle Magruder was first built by the Magruder family about 1760; the original house was incorporated into this one in about 1798. The widow's walk and dormers on the roof date from this century. One of Boucher's students at Castle Magruder was John Parke Custis, stepson of George Washington. Washington visited here at least twice, and during his studies here, Jack Custis met his future wife, Eleanor Calvert of Mount Airy. During the War of 1812, state records were moved here for safekeeping. Historic American Buildings Survey photograph; courtesy of the Library of Congress, Prints and Photographs Division

This is the graceful stair at Mount Lubentia, probably dating from 1798. Historic American Buildings Survey photograph; courtesy of the Library of Congress, Prints and Photographs Division

One of America's important colonial paintings — *The Last Supper* by Gustavus Hesselius — hangs on the choir gallery of Saint Barnabas Church. Hesselius was a Swedish-born artist who came first to Philadelphia, and then to Maryland, early in the eighteenth century. He was living in Prince George's County when he was commissioned to paint *The Last Supper* for the original brick church in 1721. Heretofore, American painting had largely been limited to portraiture; *The Last Supper* was the first major American work to depict a scene. The painting remained in the old brick church until the present structure was built; then it disappeared. It surfaced again in 1848, and for many years was on loan to the American Swedish Historical Museum and the Philadelphia Museum of Art. Its last private owner willed it once again to Queen Anne parish. Courtesy of the Philadelphia Museum of Art

There was little military activity in Prince George's County during the Revolution, but General Rochambeau's French Army passed through Bladensburg on the way north in July 1782, after wintering in Virginia following the defeat of Cornwallis at Yorktown. One of the French cartographers drew this map of the town and camp. The camp itself was in the country north of town, in what is now Hyattsville. This map was published in *The American Campaigns of Rochambeau's Army,* edited by Howard C. Rice, Jr., and Anne S. K. Brown (1972). Courtesy of Princeton University Library

General Rezin Beall (1723-1809) was one of many men from Prince George's County to serve in the Revolutionary War. His home was Turkey Flight plantation near Beltsville. Known as the "Little Man of Iron," Beall distinguished himself in fighting in Southern Maryland (repulsing early British advances in the lower Potomac) and at Harlem Heights, New York. He was buried at Turkey Flight, but in 1969 he was reinterred at Saint John's Episcopal Church in Beltsville. J. Harry Shannon photo; courtesy of the Columbia Historical Society

*J*ohn Hanson (1715-1783) patriot and statesman of the Revolution, had many ties to Prince George's County, even though he was not a Prince Georgean himself. Hanson is best remembered for his service as president of the Continental Congress, from 1781 to 1782. He is sometimes called the first president of the United States because his term was the first following the adoption of the Articles of Confederation, the nation's first plan of government. A native of Charles County and later a resident of Frederick County, Hanson married a Prince Georgean. His wife Jane was the daughter of Alexander Contee, a native of England and the progenitor of that family in Prince George's County. Hanson died while on a visit to Oxon Hill Manor and is presumed to have been buried there. His wife survived him by almost thirty years. Two of their sons died during service in the Revolutionary War. Courtesy of the Library of Congress, Prints and Photographs Division

*D*aniel Carroll II (1730-1796), a signer of the U.S. Constitution, was a native of Upper Marlboro. His father was Daniel Carroll I, a merchant from Ireland, and his mother was Eleanor Darnall, daughter of Henry Darnall II. Carroll inherited his father's mercantile business in Upper Marlboro but moved to Montgomery County (then still part of Frederick) in 1763. He was a member of both the Continental Congress and the United States Congress, a delegate to the Constitutional Convention, and one of the commissioners appointed by President Washington to lay out and plan the city of Washington. To distinguish him from several other Daniel Carrolls of the time, he is usually called Daniel Carroll the Commissioner. Courtesy of the Library of Congress, Prints and Photographs Division

*T*he first Roman Catholic bishop in the United States was John Carroll (1735-1815), a native of Upper Marlboro and brother of Daniel Carroll the commissioner. John Carroll was educated in Europe and returned to America a Jesuit priest. In 1776 he accompanied Benjamin Franklin, Samuel Chase, and his cousin, Charles Carroll of Carrollton (signer of the Declaration of Independence) to Quebec on an unsuccessful mission to seek the help of French Canadians in the Revolutionary struggle. In recognition of his leadership in the American church, Carroll was named bishop of Baltimore in 1790, and later made archbishop. He is also remembered as the founder of Georgetown University in Washington. Courtesy of the Library of Congress, Prints and Photographs Division

*T*his shows interior detail at Montpelier. Historic American Buildings Survey photograph; courtesy of the Library of Congress, Prints and Photographs Division

There is no finer home in Prince George's County than Montpelier, on the Patuxent River south of Laurel. It is a National Register Landmark. Architectural historians now believe that Montpelier dates from the 1770s or 1780s, not 1740, as was once thought. Its builders were the Snowdens, Quakers who operated iron mines and furnaces along the upper reaches of the Patuxent. The house might have been begun by Thomas Snowden (1722-1770), but it certainly was completed by his son, Major Thomas Snowden (1751-1803). Two firebacks inscribed T A S 1783 (Thomas and Anne Snowden) may indicate the completion date. Some believe the semi-octagonal wings were designed by William Buckland. Montpelier was once owned by Breckinridge Long, assistant secretary of state for presidents Woodrow Wilson and Franklin Roosevelt. It now belongs to the Maryland-National Capital Park and Planning Commission. Historic American Buildings Survey photograph; courtesy of the Library of Congress, Prints and Photographs Division

One of Maj. Thomas Snowden's visitors at Montpelier in 1800 was Abigail Adams, wife of the president, on her way to Washington. She had been advised to stay the night there, but not wanting to impose herself on strangers, proceeded on. She wrote to her sister: "We had got about a mile when we were stopped by the Major in full speed, who had learnt that I was coming on; & had kept watch for me, with his Horse at the door; as he was at a distance from the road. In the kindest, and politest manner he urged my return to his House.... There was no saying nay and I returned to a large, Handsome, Elegant House, where I was received with what we might term true English Hospitality...." (American Antiquarian Society, Worcester, Massachusetts). George Washington also visited on several occasions. In May 1787, while traveling from Mount Vernon to Philadelphia to attend the Constitutional Convention, he dined at Bladensburg and spent the night at Major Snowden's, "where feeling very severely a violent hd. ache & sick stomach I went to bed early" (Library of Congress, Manuscript Division). Courtesy of the Library of Congress, Prints and Photographs Division

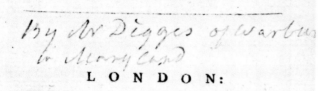

ADVENTURES

OF

ALONSO:

CONTAINING

Some STRIKING ANECDOTES of the
prefent PRIME MINISTER of POR-
TUGAL. *ie. Pombal Sebastian Jose de
Carvalho e Mello, marquis de]*

By a Native of *Maryland,* fome Years
refident in *Lifbon.*

VOL. I. and II.

*By Mr Digges of Warbur-
ton Maryland*

LONDON:

Printed for J. BEW, No. 28, Paternofter-Row.

M,DCC,LXXV.

*T*he first novel by an American was this one, *Adventures of Alonso,* published anonymously in London in 1775. Twentieth-century scholars have determined that its author was Thomas Attwood Digges of Prince George's County. Courtesy of the New York Public Library (Astor, Lenox, and Tilden foundations), Rare Books and Manuscripts Division

*T*homas Attwood Digges (1741-1821) was a most interesting character. Scion of one of the county's old Catholic families, he left Maryland as a young man and became part of the London literary and social scene in the years before the Revolutionary War. He stayed in England during the war, assisting American prisoners on behalf of the Continental Congress and secretly sending out intelligence information. He apparently diverted some of the American relief funds for his own use, however, and was roundly denounced by Benjamin Franklin. After the war, Digges engaged in industrial espionage, spiriting British industrial secrets, machinery, and even artisans out of the country and to America. He spent much time in Ireland, where he became a close friend of the Irish revolutionary Wolfe Tone. Digges returned to Maryland in the 1790s and lived at the family estate, Warburton Manor (on the Potomac), where Fort Washington was built. Some diplomatic historians have charged that late in the war Digges worked as a British agent, but Washington himself (a neighbor across the Potomac) attested to his patriotism. The portrait shown in this photograph is attributed to Sir Joshua Reynolds, but its location is now unknown. Courtesy of the Prince George's County Historical Society

The first documented balloon ascension in America took place near Bladensburg in June 1784, when Peter Carnes, an innkeeper and attorney in that town, sent an unmanned "aerostatic globe" aloft before an enthusiastic crowd. The *Virginia Journal and Alexandria Advertiser* called the grand exhibition at Bladensburg "as rich a repast as the intellectual faculties are capable of receiving." Carnes then took his balloon, which was thirty-five feet in diameter, to Baltimore, where he conducted the first manned ascension by sending a thirteen-year-old boy named Edward Warren into the air. Carnes later moved on to South Carolina and Georgia, where he became an attorney of some note. His career is summarized in *The Bench and Bar of South Carolina.* The scene in this watercolor, depicting an early French experiment, was probably similar to the scene at Bladensburg. Courtesy of the Library of Congress, Prints and Photographs Division

The building of fine homes—curtailed during the Revolution—resumed in the years after. Compton Bassett, a late Georgian masterpiece near Upper Marlboro, was built by the Hills in the 1780s to replace a house which burned in 1771. Historic American Buildings Survey photograph; courtesy of the Library of Congress, Prints and Photographs Division

Concord, on Walker Mill Road, was (and still is) a Berry home, built in the 1790s. Historic American Buildings Survey photograph; courtesy of the Library of Congress, Prints and Photographs Division

This is a recent view of Content, in Upper Marlboro. Content was built in 1787 by David Craufurd, Jr. The portion to the left is the original house; the portion on the right was added early in the nineteenth century. Many families have lived in Content, but its best-known resident was Caleb Clarke Magruder, Sr., a prominent Marlboro attorney who bought the house in 1844. Courtesy of Mr. and Mrs. Jess Joseph Smith, Jr.

This shows the chimney pent on the southern (older) side of Content. Historic American Buildings Survey photograph; courtesy of the Library of Congress, Prints and Photographs Division

*B*eall's Pleasure, in Landover, was built in 1795 by Benjamin Stoddert, who three years later became secretary of the navy. The door is topped with a brick arch and fanlight; the chair rails, cornices, hardware, and pine flooring inside are all original. This photograph was taken in 1947. Before the house are J. Whitson Rogers, Joseph Shepperd Rogers, and their pony, Blackie. Courtesy of Joseph Shepperd Rogers

*B*enjamin Stoddert (1751-1813) was called upon by President John Adams to become the nation's first secretary of the navy. A prominent Georgetown merchant, he was married to Rebecca Lowndes, daughter of Bladensburg's leading merchant, Christopher Lowndes. The Stodderts inherited Bostwick, in Bladensburg, on the death of Rebecca's mother, Elizabeth Tasker Lowndes. Benjamin Stoddert built Beall's Pleasure, on Beaverdam Creek, as a country home. Courtesy of the Library of Congress, Prints and Photographs Division

The Stoddert children, Elizabeth, Harriet, and Benjamin, were painted by Charles Willson Peale at Georgetown in 1789. Elizabeth became the mother of Confederate general Richard Stoddert Ewell; Harriet married George Washington Campbell, United States senator, secretary of the treasury, and minister to Russia. This painting hangs in Dumbarton House, Washington, the property of the National Society of the Colonial Dames of America. Courtesy of the National Portrait Gallery

The old Riggs Mill—now known as the Adelphi Mill—is the largest (and probably the oldest) surviving mill in the metropolitan Washington area. The mill and nearby miller's cottage were built on the Northwest Branch by Issachar and Mahlon Scholfield about 1796, when they had several tracts of land resurveyed and renamed Adelphi. The Riggs family owned the mill from the time of the Civil War until the 1920s. Now restored, it is owned by the Maryland-National Capital Park and Planning Commission and is used for community meetings. Historic American Buildings Survey photograph; courtesy of the Library of Congress, Prints and Photographs Division

Throughout the Revolution and the immediate postwar period, Congress and the government of the United States moved from city to city. Finally, in 1790 Congress agreed to build a permanent capital and directed President Washington to choose a site somewhere along the Potomac River. The site he chose was in Prince George's County. In this painting by Edward Savage, President and Mrs. Washington and their grandchildren are portrayed with a map of the federal city. The Eastern Branch (the Anacostia River) is in the foreground. Courtesy of the National Gallery of Art

President Washington engaged Major Pierre L'Enfant, a French engineer and architect, to plan the city. L'Enfant came to America early in the Revolutionary War, became an officer with the Corps of Engineers, and stayed here after the war. This is his plan for the city, engraved by Andrew Ellicott, as it appeared in the *Universal Asylum and Columbian Magazine* for March 1792. L'Enfant took particular care in selecting the site of the Capitol, writing, "I could find no one [site] to greet the congressional building as is that on the west end of Jenkins heights...." He called Jenkins Hill—now Capitol Hill—a pedestal waiting for a monument.

Pierre L'Enfant was a temperamental man who disliked supervision and ignored deadlines; President Washington and the city commissioners found it difficult to work with him. Despite L'Enfant's genius, President Washington was eventually forced to dismiss him. Twenty-two years later, in 1814, L'Enfant was again engaged by the government, this time to design a fort on the Potomac River—now Fort Washington. The same problems arose, and again he was dismissed. He spent his final years with the Digges family of Prince George's County, first with Thomas Attwood Digges at Warburton Manor (site of Fort Washington) and then with William Dudley Digges at Chilham Castle Manor, in the northwest corner of the county. There he died in 1825. L'Enfant was buried at Chilham Castle Manor but was reinterred in 1909 at Arlington National Cemetery, overlooking the city he designed. Courtesy of the Library of Congress, Prints and Photographs Division

Congress intended the federal city to be part of a federal district ten miles square. President Washington hired a Baltimore County surveyor, Andrew Ellicott, to survey the district and mark its boundaries. Working with Ellicott was Benjamin Banneker, a free black who was an astronomer and mathematician. This portrait is taken from the title page of an almanac Banneker published in 1795. Courtesy of the Prince George's County Historical Society

Boundary stones were set at mile intervals to mark the boundary between the District of Columbia and Maryland. Seventeen were placed between Prince George's County and the District of Columbia, and most are still in place. This is Northeast No. 8, located in the woods near Kenilworth Avenue. Courtesy of the D.C. Public Library

*T*obacco leaves adorn the columns of the Capitol, a reminder that the city of Washington was once Prince George's County tobacco land. Courtesy of the Architect of the Capitol and the Library of Congress

Chapter 5

ANTEBELLUM PRINCE GEORGE'S COUNTY

If thou wouldst view fair Melrose aright,
Go visit it by the pale moonlight;
For the gay beams of lightsome day
Gild, but to flout, the ruins gray.

Sir Walter Scott
"The Lay of the Last Minstrel"

With his ancient tales of bravery and valor, chivalry and romance, Sir Walter Scott was one of the favorite poets of the antebellum South. The Southerners of that day saw themselves in his poems, for as W. J. Cash has written in *The Mind of the South,* they believed their society to be the last great realm of chivalry in the world. Later generations of Southerners, living in harder times, looked back upon the prewar years as a golden age. To the modern conscience, a society based upon slave labor cannot be called a golden one, yet there was a romance about the Old South, a South of which Prince George's County was very much a part.

There was great wealth in Prince George's County in the years before the Civil War, wealth that came from the land, from tobacco, and from slaves. Prince George's County was the greatest tobacco-producing county in Maryland. More slaves worked here than in any other county in the state, and the gentry, the old families who led our social and public life, lived in a style befitting the legends that linger about them. The romantics say that Prince George's County was a grand and gracious place then, an important place, and they are right, it was. But Prince George's County was not important because of the style the romantics so admire. There was substantial achievement along with the style. In no other age have Prince Georgeans played such conspicuous roles in state and national affairs. In no other age have Prince Georgeans contributed so much to the advancement of agriculture, the foundation upon which the economy here rested for more than two hundred years. The Prince Georgeans of the antebellum era built

institutions their forefathers never did: banks, newpapers, small industries, and associations of every kind. Prince Georgeans were confident in those years. If the county had an image then, it was one of leadership and innovation, as well as wealth and style.

Prince George's leadership in state and national affairs actually began before the antebellum era, in the first years of the Union. Daniel Carroll, a native of Upper Marlboro, participated in the deliberations of the Constitutional Convention and became a signer of that document. His brother, John Carroll, founded Georgetown University and became the first Roman Catholic bishop (and later archbishop) in the United States. Thomas John Claggett of Croom played an important role in the organization of the Protestant Episcopal Church after the Revolution and became the first Episcopal bishop consecrated in this country. Thomas Sim Lee, Benjamin Ogle, Robert Bowie, Samuel Sprigg, Joseph Kent, and Thomas Pratt all became governors of Maryland. Benjamin Stoddert became the first secretary of the navy, William Wirt (a native of Bladensburg) became attorney general of the United States, and Gabriel Duvall sat for twenty-three years on the United States Supreme Court.

Prince Georgeans were also in the forefront of the agricultural research movement that developed early in the nineteenth century. Dr. John H. Bayne, a physician, gained a national reputation as the "prince of horticulturalists." W. W. W. Bowie, a tobacco planter near Collington, wrote extensively for agricultural journals and government publications. Charles Benedict Calvert of Riversdale conducted all sorts of agricultural experiments on his plantation; led county, state, and national agricultural societies; and lobbied hard for the creation of the U.S. Department of Agriculture. The University of Maryland at College Park is his monument, for he was the leader of the planters who founded the Maryland Agricultural College, as it was first known, in 1856. One of the earliest agricultural colleges in the nation, it was built upon Calvert's Ross Borough Farm, part of the great Riversdale estate.

Prince George's County was witness to technological as well as agricultural advancement in the antebellum era. In 1835 one of the first rail lines in the country, the Washington branch of the Baltimore and Ohio Railroad, was built through Prince George's County. Coming from Baltimore, the line entered the county at Laurel and ran southwesterly to Bladensburg, then into Washington. The first trains to enter Washington—and pass through Prince George's County—were greeted with much fanfare. "It was a glorious sight," reported the *National Intelligencer* on August 26, 1835, "to see four trains of cars, with each its engine, extending altogether several hundred yards in length, making their entry by this new route...." The rail line immediately brought about the birth of a new community called Beltsville. The Baltimore and Ohio Railroad established a rail stop and freight depot on land purchased from Trueman Belt, and they named the place for him. Beltsville was doubly blessed, for the Baltimore-Washington Turnpike crossed the rail line there. It soon became a thriving little trading center, eclipsing the older community of Vansville further north on the pike. Beltsville would not be the only community the railroad would spawn. Later in that century, all along the line, residential towns would be built, the first of Washington's suburbs in Prince George's County.

The second technological marvel Prince Georgeans saw developed in the antebellum years was the telegraph. Samuel F. B. Morse, working under a congressional appropriation, conducted early experiments at Riversdale, the plantation of Charles Benedict Calvert of agricultural renown. On April 9, 1844, the first experimental telegraph message into Washington was sent from Riversdale, from a point on the rail line. Several weeks later, on May 24, the famous telegraph message from the U.S. Capitol— "What hath God wrought"—coursed its way through wires strung along the railroad all the way to Baltimore. It was the first intercity telegraph communication in America.

During the antebellum years, Prince George's County was touched by the Industrial Revolution. Early in the nineteenth century Nicholas Snowden of Montpelier built a large grist mill by the side of the Patuxent River. Larger than any other mill in Prince George's County, it was converted into a cotton mill in the 1820s, spinning cotton yarn with power provided

by the falling Patuxent. Soon a loom was installed, and then, in the 1830s, the railroad was built nearby. By the 1840s several hundred people lived around the mill and a town was born, named for the greenery in the vicinity: Laurel. The railroad, the power of the river, and the town's location midway between Baltimore and Washington encouraged other industries to locate there, and Laurel flourished. It was an anomaly in Prince George's County, a town whose base was industry instead of agriculture. Laurel has always stood apart, and been somewhat different from the rest of the county; to this day that is true. For decades Laurel was the largest town in Prince George's County, until the residential suburban towns near Washington surpassed it in population.

Into this narrative of wealth and style, leadership and innovation, must be inserted the story of the county's greatest embarrassment, the Battle of Bladensburg. The battle took place in 1814, during the final year of the War of 1812. Americans were fighting the British for the second time. As in the previous war, British ships in the Chesapeake harassed Maryland, but without invasion, until British troops on the European continent were suddenly freed for American duty by the defeat of Napoleon. Then they came to Maryland in large numbers. They entered the Chesapeake, sailed up the Patuxent River, and marched overland through Prince George's County to Nottingham, Upper Marlboro, Long Old Fields (Forestville), and then to Bladensburg. There, on August 24, 1814, on the grounds and heights to the west of town, they met an untrained and ill-prepared defensive force of Maryland and District of Columbia militia. The defenders were no match for the British army. After a brief engagement they scattered, all except a contingent of 500 regular American marines and sailors led by

Commodore Joshua Barney. They fought valiantly, but with no support were forced to retreat, too. The flight left Washington unguarded, and the victorious British marched into the city and burned it. The battle was a rout, and a profound embarrassment to President Madison, who was on hand to witness the sad affair with most of his cabinet. Fortunately, the taking of Washington had little military significance, for the British departed the next day. The successful defense of Baltimore a few weeks later—at Hampstead Hill and Fort McHenry—restored American pride, but for years the very name Bladensburg was synonymous with national humiliation.

As the nineteenth century passed its midpoint, the plantation economy of Prince George's County was at the height of its development. By 1860 the county was producing more than thirteen million pounds of tobacco annually, more than twice as much as Calvert or Anne Arundel. Tobacco was not the only crop raised here, though: farmers produced more than 300,000 bushels of wheat and about 700,000 bushels of corn, and owned 5,000 horses, 4,000 milk cows, 9,000 sheep, and 25,000 swine.

Much of the farm work in the county was done by slaves, of course. Among the 2,000 white families in the county there were 850 slaveholders, holding 12,500 slaves. Half of the slaveholders held fewer than ten slaves, and 145 held only one, but there were 50 slaveholders who owned more than 50 slaves. None held more than 200. Not all blacks were slaves, however. There was also a small free black population, to the number of 1,198 in 1860. Most of the free blacks were small farmers or laborers, although a very few, like John Cooper early in the century, acquired some measure of wealth. Cooper, who died in 1815, owned a plantation of more than 100 acres in the Forestville area. Perhaps the largest of the free black families in Prince George's County before the Civil War were the Queens, most of whom lived near Queen Anne.

The white population of the county—totaling 9,650 in 1860—was mostly of British stock, and the early colonial distinctions between the Scots, English, and Irish had faded with intermarriage over the years. While they had not increased their numbers in at least seventy years—which meant that many sons and daughters left Prince George's to make a living—it seemed not to affect the overall economy, as long as slaves continued to labor in the tobacco fields. According to the United States census, there were sixteen Methodist churches here, fourteen Episcopalian, four Catholic, and one struggling Presbyterian church at Bladensburg—the lineal descendant of Ninian Beall's Upper Marlboro church of 1704. Most of the descendants of those early Scots had become Episcopalians!

The politics of this county were markedly conservative in the antebellum period, and the voters usually elected Whigs to local office. There was virtually no sympathy at all—among the whites—for the radical tenets of abolitionism, and the leaders of Prince George's were firm in their defense of the slave system. Thomas J. Turner was publisher of *The Planters' Advocate,* an Upper Marlboro newspaper begun in 1851. In the inaugural issue he wrote, "We believe domestic slavery, as it exists among us, to be a truly conservative and beneficial institution—right in view of God and man, and as such, we will ever maintain it." He expressed well the sentiments of most Prince Georgeans. But within fifteen years, the system and society he vowed to maintain forever would come crashing down in ruins.

Then go—but go alone the while—
Then view St. David's ruin'd pile;
And, home returning, soothly swear
Was never a scene so sad and fair!

Stagecoaches once traveled the old Washington and Baltimore Turnpike through Prince George's County — now a public road known as Route One. This print depicts a scene near Vansville about 1830 in the heyday of stage travel, when it took five hours to make the trip between the two cities. The Baltimore and Ohio Railroad — built in the 1830s parallel to the road — eventually put the stage line out of business. Courtesy of the Maryland Historical Society, Baltimore

The Rossborough Inn was built about 1803 a few miles north of Bladensburg to serve travelers on the road between Washington and Baltimore. In 1858 it became part of the Maryland Agricultural College (now the University of Maryland) and served a variety of purposes until it was restored in the 1930s. Since 1954 the inn has been the home of the university's faculty club. Carved on the keystone above the door is the head of Silenus, son of Pan and teacher of Bacchus. Courtesy of the Prince George's County, Maryland, Conference and Visitors Bureau, Inc.

*M*attaponi, near Croom, was the home of Governor Robert Bowie, inherited from his father. He also owned another home, later known as the Cedars, in the town of Nottingham. Governor Bowie was an ardent Jeffersonian, and a sign once outside Mattaponi proclaimed it the home of Maryland's first radical governor. The porch, the stucco, and the tiny dormer have been removed since this photograph was taken in the 1930s, giving the house the appearance of a formal mansion. The building date is uncertain, but is traditionally given as 1745, with alterations and wings added in 1820. Mattaponi is now owned by the Catholic Church. Historic American Buildings Survey photograph; courtesy of the Library of Congress, Prints and Photographs Division

*R*obert Bowie (1750-1818) served as governor of Maryland from 1803 to 1806 and from 1811 to 1812. He was a resident of Prince George's County. Courtesy of the Maryland Commission on Artistic Property

*R*osalie Eugenia Stier (1778-1821) was born near Antwerp; she married George Calvert in 1799, five years after her family came to America. This portrait was painted by Gilbert Stuart in 1805. With Rosalie is her oldest child, Caroline Maria, who later became Mrs. Thomas Willing Morris of Philadelphia. Courtesy of the Maryland Historical Society, Baltimore

*G*eorge Calvert (1768-1838), a descendant of the Lords Baltimore, was the son of Benedict Calvert of Mount Airy. He and his wife Rosalie had nine children. Their oldest son was the noted author George Henry Calvert, also mayor of Newport, Rhode Island; their second son was Charles Benedict Calvert, agriculturalist and Congressman. This portrait of George Calvert was painted by Gilbert Stuart. Courtesy of the Maryland Historical Society, Baltimore

*R*iversdale, a brick Georgian mansion covered with stucco, was built a few miles north of Bladensburg by Baron Henri Joseph Stier, a Belgian nobleman who fled the French Revolution. Stier began work in 1801 but returned to Europe in 1803. His daughter Rosalie and her American husband, George Calvert, finished the house. It remained in the Calvert family until 1887. The town of Riverdale was later built around the mansion. Photograph by the author

*T*his is Melford, near Bowie. It was built about 1810 or shortly thereafter and was a Duckett home during most of the nineteenth century. The two-story, semicircular brick bay on the south side of the house is unique in the architecture of Prince George's County. Historic American Buildings Survey photograph; courtesy of the Library of Congress, Prints and Photographs Division

*T*his is Addison Chapel, an old Episcopal church situated atop a hill above Addison Road in Seat Pleasant. There is no church building in Prince George's County with a more enigmatic history than this one. The county's Historic Sites and Districts Plan recognizes a building date between 1809 and 1816; other sources offer dates of 1746 and the 1760s. Whatever the case, this hill has been a site of worship since 1696, when Colonel John Addison erected a log chapel here for his tenants on nearby lands. Many prominent Prince Georgeans have worshipped on this hill; the graves of Benjamin Stoddert, his wife, Rebecca Lowndes, and her father, Christopher Lowndes, are in the foreground of this photograph. In 1902 the pitch of the roof was changed and the interior remodeled. Addison Chapel no longer has an active congregation, but its ancient cemetery is an oasis of calm above busy Addison Road. Photo by the author

Gabriel Duvall probably began building his home, Marietta, around 1810. A wing, behind this main block, was added about 1830; a second, in this century. Justice Duvall's law office is at the far right; the other structure is a root cellar. This photo was taken in 1893. Marietta is located on Bell Station Road near Glenn Dale and is now owned by the Maryland-National Capital Park and Planning Commission. It serves as the headquarters and library of the Prince George's County Historical Society. Courtesy of the Maryland-National Capital Park and Planning Commission, History Division

Gabriel Duvall (1752-1844) became a justice of the United States Supreme Court in 1812 after a long and varied career in public and political service, including two terms in Congress. He served on the court until 1835. A native of Prince George's County, he lived many years in Annapolis before building a new home on his family estate near Glenn Dale. Courtesy of the Library of Congress, Prints and Photographs Division

On August 24, 1814—during the third year of the War of 1812—British troops under the command of Major General Robert Ross entered the city of Washington and burned the Capitol, the White House, and other public and private buildings. The capture of the city had no military significance—the British left the very next day—but the defeat was a humiliating one for the United States. This illustration shows the way a British almanac portrayed the battle for Washington, but the battle was really nothing like this. The American defense actually took place at Bladensburg, in a battle most Americans have chosen to forget. Courtesy of the Library of Congress, Prints and Photographs Division

On August 19, 1814, approximately 4,500 British infantrymen, artillerymen, and marines left their ships at Benedict, on the Patuxent River. Their immediate orders were to take Commodore Joshua Barney's American flotilla, trapped further up the river—but nearby Washington, the capital of the young republic, proved too tempting a prize to resist. The British proceeded slowly across Prince George's County, encountered virtually no resistance, and encamped at Nottingham, Upper Marlboro, and Melwood before making the irrevocable decision to proceed on to Washington. They assumed the lower bridges of the Anacostia would be burned, so they headed to Bladensburg, where they could ford the river if necessary. This map of the march appeared in the book *Campaigns of the War of 1812-15 Against Great Britain,* by George Washington Cullum (1879).

American troops under General William Henry Winder were also active in Prince George's County between August 19 and 24, making camp at The Woodyard and Long Old Fields (Forestville). Winder had 3,000 men at Long Old Fields and planned to attack the British at Upper Marlboro, but when the enemy advanced to Melwood, he withdrew to Washington. When he finally learned that the British were heading for Bladensburg, he decided to make his stand there. Courtesy of the Library of Congress

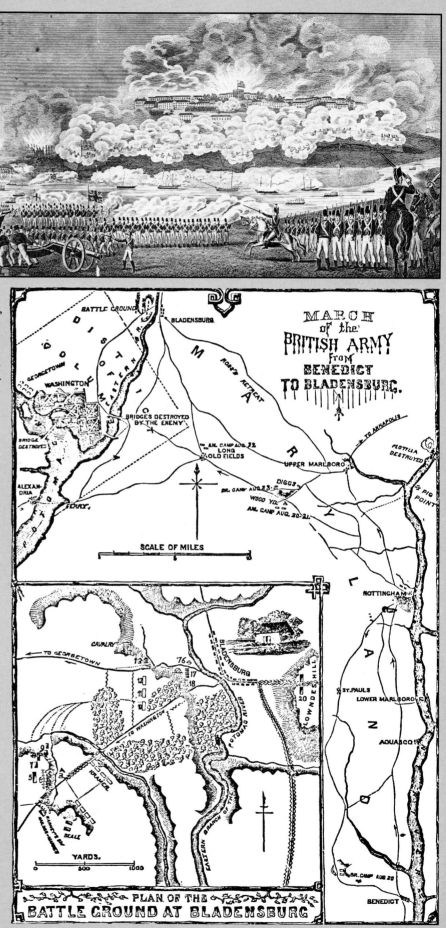

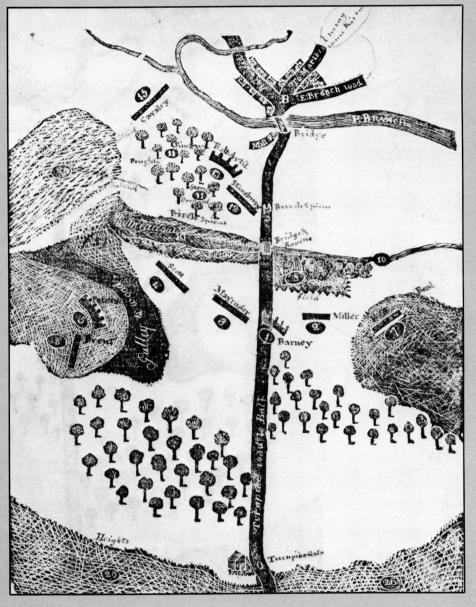

The American force that met the British at Bladensburg numbered about 6,000, but they were mostly inexperienced militiamen from the District and Maryland. Bladensburg itself was abandoned; the troops were positioned across the river on both sides of the road to Washington (now Bladensburg Road). As the British marched down Lowndes Hill into the town, the American fire began. But the Americans would be no match for the experienced British troops and the terror of the Congreve rockets. The Battle of Bladensburg was a rout, and the Americans fled. This map (with Bladensburg at the top and the District line at the bottom) shows the positions of the American defenders. From *A Narrative of the Battle of Bladensburg* by Thomas Parker (1814). Courtesy of the Library of Congress, Prints and Photographs Division

*A*fter scattering the American defenders at Bladensburg, the British entered the city of Washington unimpeded. Among the many buildings they burned was the Capitol. Courtesy of the Library of Congress, Prints and Photographs Division

Commodore Joshua Barney—a Marylander—was the only American hero to emerge from the debacle at Bladensburg. He was the commander of the American ships in the Patuxent that were the first object of the British advance. After destroying his flotilla (to prevent its capture), he brought his 500 men to Washington. On the day of the battle they were assigned to hold the center of the American line. They fought valiantly, leaving the field only after everyone else had retreated. Barney himself was wounded and captured, but in that very different age, was treated with the utmost respect and courtesy by his captors. He was released the same day. Courtesy of the Library of Congress, Prints and Photographs Division

President James Madison was present at the Battle of Bladensburg, wearing a pair of dueling pistols lent him by Secretary of the Treasury George Campbell, Benjamin Stoddert's son-in-law. Several members of the cabinet were also there— Secretary of State James Monroe, Secretary of War John Armstrong, and Attorney General Richard Rush. The president was well in front of the American lines—almost at the bridge—when the British reached town; at one point a lone American scout galloping full-speed down Lowndes Hill was all that stood between him and the British army. After a quick retreat back to the lines, the president and his party accepted the American commander's advice to retire to the rear. Courtesy of the Library of Congress, Prints and Photographs Division

Bladensburg Races.

WRITTEN SHORTLY AFTER THE CAPTURE OF

WASHINGTON CITY,

August 24, 1814.

⟨Probably it is not generally known, that the flight of MAHOMET, the flight of JOHN GILPIN, and the flight of BLADENS-BURG, all occurred on the *twenty-fourth of August.*⟩

PRINTED FOR THE PURCHASER

1816.

The field at Bladensburg is shown many years later. The ravine soon gained a notoriety of its own, for nearly fifty duels were fought there in the years between the battle and the Civil War. Among the men to fall at those "dark and bloody grounds" was the naval hero Stephen Decatur, killed on March 22, 1820. Located just beyond the District of Columbia line, it was a convenient place for the gentlemen of Washington to settle their quarrels, beyond the reach of federal law. The Bladensburg dueling grounds are now part of a park and lie between the town of Colmar Manor and the Fort Lincoln Cemetery. Courtesy of the Library of Congress, Prints and Photographs Division

A long poem—published by opponents of the Madison administration—ridiculed the president's hasty retreat and the government's conduct of the war. "The Bladensburg Races" became the name by which the battle was remembered. Courtesy of the Enoch Pratt Free Library, Baltimore

General Leonard Covington (1768-1813), a native of Prince George's County, was killed during the War of 1812 at the Battle of Sackett's Harbor, New York. Covington was born at Aquasco, the family plantation on the Patuxent River. After the death of his wife and only child, Covington became an officer in the U.S. Army, serving from 1792 to 1795 and again from 1809 until his death. He was elected to the state senate and the United States Congress during the break in his military career. His was an old Prince George's County family; his great-grandfather, Levin Covington, was a justice of the county court and built the first courthouse in Upper Marlboro.

In 1810, while in command of troops near Natchez, Mississippi, Leonard Covington acquired a plantation he named Propinquity. There he intended to settle permanently, near Covington, Wailes, and Magruder kinsmen from Prince George's County. A good many Prince Georgeans moved to the old Southwest during the antebellum era; they also settled in Kentucky, Missouri, and Texas in large numbers. This portrait of Leonard Covington appeared in *Memoir of Leonard Covington,* written by B. L. C. Wailes in 1861 and published in 1928. Courtesy of C. Segrest Wailes

On August 28, after returning to their ships, the British sent a party back to Upper Marlboro to seize Dr. William Beanes, a prominent resident of that town. Along with former governor Robert Bowie, Beanes had led a small force of Prince Georgeans who had captured and jailed several British stragglers. The British, in turn, seized Bowie, Beanes, and several other townspeople as hostages. When the British stragglers were released, so were the Americans—all except Dr. Beanes, who was taken to Baltimore. The government sent Francis Scott Key (a Georgetown lawyer from an old Maryland family) to the British to negotiate for the release of Dr. Beanes. There, with Beanes, he witnessed the bombardment of Fort McHenry and was inspired to write "The Star Spangled Banner," our national anthem. This is one of many likenesses of Francis Scott Key; there are no known extant portraits of Dr. Beanes. The doctor and his wife were buried in Upper Marlboro on the schoolhouse hill high above town. Courtesy of the Library of Congress, Prints and Photographs Division

*W*eston is a large plantation located along Crain Highway southwest of Upper Marlboro. Captain Thomas Clagett, immigrant—whose grandfathers were mayors of London and Canterbury—acquired the land late in the seventeenth century: three hundred years and eight generations later it is still a Clagett home. The first house at Weston was built about 1702; it burned during the Revolution and was replaced by another; that one burned in 1816 and was replaced by this house. This house was built by the sixth Thomas Clagett; his great-grandson lives there now. Historic American Buildings Survey photograph; courtesy of the Library of Congress, Prints and Photographs Division

*S*amuel Sprigg (1783-1855) was a native of Prince George's County who served as governor of Maryland from 1819 to 1822. He lived at Northampton, a plantation in the central part of the county. Courtesy of the Maryland Commission on Artistic Property

Perhaps no home better symbolizes the spirit of the antebellum era than Bowieville, one of the finest examples of Federal-style architecture in the county. Bowieville was built in the early 1820s by Mary Bowie, daughter of Governor Robert Bowie and widow of Turner Wootton and Thomas Contee Bowie. "She is described as a woman of masculine business capacity and energy, who managed her large plantation with skill and success," wrote Effie Gwynn Bowie in *Across the Years in Prince George's County.* Mary Bowie died in 1825 at the age of fifty-five. Bowieville is located along Church Road, south of Central Avenue. It awaits restoration. Historic American Buildings Survey photograph; courtesy of the Library of Congress, Prints and Photographs Division

This is an interior view of Bowieville, taken in the 1930s. The house is also noted for its mantles of black marble and beautiful ceiling medallions. There are many who say that there is no other home in Prince George's County as handsome inside as this one. Historic American Buildings Survey photograph; courtesy of the Library of Congress, Prints and Photographs Division

This is an 1822 receipt for the deposit of hogsheads of tobacco at the Queen Anne warehouse. The receipt states quantity and quality. The Sophia Duckett named was probably Sophia (Mullikin) Duckett, wife of Basil Duckett and daughter of Belt Mullikin. Courtesy of the Prince George's County Historical Society

Patuxent River, Queen Anne Warehouse, June 19th 1822

RECEIVED of Sophia Duckett Five Hogsheads of Tobacco, Mark, Number, and Weight, as per Margin, which I promise to deliver to the said Duckett or bearer for exportation, when demanded.

Inspector.

Mark.	No.	Gross.	Tare.	Net.
SD	1101	882	128	754
	1102	829	122	707
	1103	832	119	773
	1104	873	122	751
	1105	784	122	662

Dr. Joseph Kent (1779-1837), of Prince George's County, was governor of Maryland from 1826 to 1829. A native of Calvert County, he lived at Rose Mount, near Landover. Courtesy of the Maryland Commission on Artistic Property

Overlooking the Potomac River in southern Prince George's County is Fort Washington, ten miles downriver from Washington, D.C. Completed in 1824, it replaced an earlier fort (Fort Warburton) built in 1809 and destroyed during the War of 1812 to prevent it from falling into British hands. The point on which Fort Washington and its predecessor were built was once part of the Digges family plantation, Warburton Manor. Mount Vernon is right across the river, and George Washington dined often with the Digges family at Warburton house. This was Fort Washington about 1880, as seen in an old print. Courtesy of the D.C. Public Library

This watercolor of the mill at Upper Marlboro, by John H. B. Latrobe, was published in 1827 in the *Progressive Drawing Book*. The mill stood by Old Mill Road along Federal Spring Branch. This watercolor is one of the earliest depictions of a scene in Prince George's County. Courtesy of the Enoch Pratt Free Library, Baltimore

*H*oly Trinity at Collington was built in 1836 on the site of an earlier Episcopal chapel established by the Reverend Jacob Henderson about 1712. There have been several additions to the church since it was first built; the narthex was added to the south front in 1921. A brick rectory built in the 1820s stands near the church. Built by tobacco planters, Holy Trinity today serves the Episcopalians of the city of Bowie. Historic American Buildings Survey photograph; courtesy of the Library of Congress, Prints and Photographs Division

*W*illiam Wirt (1772-1834), a native of Bladensburg, served as attorney general of the United States for twelve years (1817-1829), the longest tenure of any individual in that office. He moved to Virginia as a young man, and first attracted national attention as prosecutor in the Aaron Burr treason trial. In 1832 he was the presidential candidate of the Anti-Masonic Party, though he carried only the state of Vermont in the general election. Wirt was a noted essayist as well as a lawyer and politician. His father owned the Indian Queen Tavern in Bladensburg. Courtesy of the Library of Congress, Prints and Photographs Division

*S*alubria, on Oxon Hill Road, was built about 1830 by Dr. John H. Bayne (1804-1870), a physician and one of the most influential leaders in Prince George's County in the middle years of the nineteenth century. He was elected this county's state senator in 1861, and though a slaveholder, was a firm Unionist. He foresaw the inevitable end of slavery and became one of the few here to speak out in favor of emancipation (*Marlboro Gazette*, 30 March 1864). After the war, Dr. Bayne became president of the county school board, directing the development of the new public school system. Tragedy, alas, was no stranger to his family. On November 6, 1834, a deranged fourteen-year-old slave girl named Judith poisoned Dr. Bayne's two young sons with arsenic from her master's pharmacy. Both died within days. She further confessed to causing the death of Dr. Bayne's infant daughter two years before. Judith was tried at Upper Marlboro, found guilty, and hanged. Historic American Buildings Survey photograph; courtesy of the Library of Congress, Prints and Photographs Division

*T*he public school system of Prince George's County, as it exists today, was not established until after the Civil War. There were, however, a number of private and locally supported schools before the war. This was one of them. This school was built early in the nineteenth century on the corner of Edmonston and Annapolis roads in Bladensburg. It was known as the Bladensburg Academy, and was the successor of a private academy founded in colonial times. The Bladensburg Academy eventually became part of the public school system and stood until the first decade of this century. The site is still dedicated to the cause of education; the county library maintains a branch in the old primary school (built in 1925) that stands there now. Courtesy of the Prince George's County Historical Society

The first railroad line to traverse Prince George's County, the Washington branch of the Baltimore and Ohio Railroad, opened in 1835. It entered the county at Laurel and passed through Bladensburg on its way to Washington. One of the oldest rail lines in the nation, it is still in operation today, carrying commuters and freight through Laurel, Beltsville, College Park, Riverdale, and Hyattsville. This pen-and-ink drawing was made by Augustus Kollner in 1839 and shows an early train just inside the District line. Most of the District of Columbia was, of course, still farmland then. Courtesy of the Library of Congress, Prints and Photographs Division

Mr Jo Wood

To Owners of Steam Boat Patuxent,

1835.

To Freight from Baltimore to Patuxent, on

May 15

1 Bundle Books — 18 7/4

J Point   Received payment.

Steamboats first came to Patuxent and Potomac waters in the 1810s and 1820s. They carried tobacco from Prince George's County to Baltimore for more than 100 years, until good roads and highways made truck transport more convenient. They also brought back all sorts of goods in return. Thomas Wood lived at the plantation East View, near Aquasco. The town was then known as Woodville, for his family. The business records of East View are preserved in the Maryland Historical Society in Baltimore. Courtesy of the Maryland Historical Society, Baltimore

106

*R*epresentative of Prince George's County's early industry is the Avondale Mill, built in Laurel in 1845. Destroyed by fire in 1991, it was the last of Laurel's nineteenth-century mills to survive. The site is now a city park. Built for the manufacture of cotton cloth, it became a grist mill ten years later, but was used as a lace factory for a few years early in the twentieth century. It was sometimes known as Crabbs Flour Mill for a nineteenth-century owner, B. F. Crabbs. The mill stood one block off Main Street on the banks of the Patuxent River—the source of its power. This photograph was taken by Robert H. Sadler, Jr., in the early years of the twentieth century. Courtesy of Dr. Robert S. McCeney and John C. Brennan

*H*orace Capron (1804-1885) was one of the county's early industrialists. A native of Massachusetts, he grew up in New York and entered the cotton manufacturing business. He was working at a mill in Baltimore County when in 1834 he married Louisa Snowden, whose father, Nicholas, established the Snowden mills in Laurel. Within two years Capron was managing the Snowden mills, and under his direction the operations were greatly expanded. Louisa Snowden Capron died in 1849, and in 1852 Capron left Maryland to serve as an Indian agent in Texas. He remarried and settled in Illinois, and during the Civil War served as an officer of Illinois volunteers.

Capron was an agriculturalist as well as an industrialist; he was United States commissioner of agriculture (predecessor of the secretary of agriculture) between 1867 and 1871. His statue stands prominently in the city of Sapporo, Japan, a monument to the work he did on the island of Hokkaido as an advisor on agricultural development, from 1871 to 1875. Capron's career is more fully treated in the *Dictionary of American Biography.* This photograph was taken by Mathew Brady during the Civil War. Courtesy of the National Archives

*I*n August 1845, *The American Farmer* reported that Mr. Capron had erected a number of "two story stone houses, each competent for four families" as homes for mill workers. A number of those houses survive to this day, and they are affectionately called the "old ladies" of Laurel. This is one of them.

The American Farmer held up Laurel as a model of what an industrial town could be, and recommended the establishment of other such towns across the agricultural South. "There are but few neighborhoods where factories might be established, where numerous poor white families might not be found, to whom such employment would be highly beneficial." It concluded: "We left Laurel with the impression that it was one of the best arranged communities we had ever been in, and the loveliest spot which we had ever beheld." Many of the mill workers, incidentally, were women, of whom *The American Farmer* wrote: "We do not believe that the same number of females can be selected anywhere, whether in country, or town, whose appearance and deportment would be more indicative of good health and sound morals." *Washington Star* photo; copyright *Washington Post*; reprinted by permission of the D.C. Public Library

108

*H*itching Post Hill—also known as Ash Hill—is a Greek Revival home near Hyattsville. It was built about 1840 by Robert Clark, an Englishman. General Edward Fitzgerald Beale bought the estate in 1875; he entertained Presidents Grant and Cleveland, as well as Buffalo Bill Cody, here. Beale was an associate of Kit Carson and a pathfinder of the Old West. He traveled across the country six times in two years during the 1840s. Bayard Taylor called him the "pioneer in the path of empire," and Charles Nordhoff described him as "a sparkling combination of scholar, gentleman, and Indian fighter." He became the United States minister to Austria-Hungary in 1876. Beale also owned the Decatur House on Lafayette Square in Washington, as well as the huge Rancho Tejon near Bakersfield, California. Courtesy of Mr. and Mrs. John Giannetti

*L*ocust Grove, in Beltsville, also dated from the antebellum period. It was the home of the Emack family for 100 years, before commercial development along Route One took it away in the 1940s. This handsome house was attached to another, a much older one, which became a rear wing. Two Emack sons from Locust Grove became Confederate officers during the Civil War. George Malcolm sustained several wounds; James William was killed at Chancellorsville. Courtesy of the Prince George's County Historical Society

*T*rinity Episcopal Church in Upper Marlboro dates from the 1840s, but the land on which it stands has been dedicated to God's work since 1704, when Colonel Ninian Beall deeded the site to the county's first Presbyterian congregation. The Presbyterians of Upper Marlboro worshipped here until their congregation was absorbed by Bladensburg's late in the eighteenth century; the town's Episcopalians then acquired the old wooden Presbyterian church and made it their own. They built this brick church in 1846; the tower was added in 1896. Courtesy of Prince George's County, Maryland, Conference and Visitors Bureau, Inc.

*T*homas G. Pratt (1804-1869) was governor of Maryland from 1845 to 1848. He lived in Upper Marlboro and later became a United States senator. Courtesy of the Maryland Commission on Artistic Property

*R*everdy Johnson (1796-1876), a United States senator, attorney general, and minister to Great Britain, had many ties to Prince George's County. A native of Anne Arundel County, he was the son of John Johnson, Sr., and Deborah Ghiselin. His father was judge of the state court of appeals and chancellor of Maryland; his mother's brother, Dr. Reverdy Ghiselin, married Margaret Anne Bowie (daughter of Governor Robert Bowie) and established the Ghiselin name in this county. After graduating from Saint John's College in Annapolis, Reverdy Johnson began the practice of law in Upper Marlboro. Like his uncle, he married a Bowie: Mary Mackall Bowie, a granddaughter of the governor. The young couple moved to Baltimore, where Johnson embarked on his long career in politics.

Reverdy Johnson was associated with two historic sites in this county. The first was Williams Plains, a fine old home near Bowie built by his father about 1813; the other was his law office in Upper Marlboro, now destroyed. "Until a few years ago," wrote Effie Gwynn Bowie in 1947, "the little brick law office of Reverdy Johnson stood at the corner of Main and Water streets and was one of the really interesting places in the village. It was removed to make place for the Marlboro Implement Company's building, to the regret of the older people of the community." Courtesy of the Library of Congress, Prints and Photographs Division

*A*n interesting old home from the antebellum period was the Octagon House. It stood along the Northeast Branch opposite Bladensburg, on what is now Forty-second Place in Hyattsville. The Octagon House was built about 1853 by Henry T. Scott, a druggist in Bladensburg. The octagon style was popular then; it was first promoted by Orson S. Fowler in a book he published in 1848 entitled *A Home for All.* The house was destroyed many years ago. Courtesy of the Prince George's County Historical Society

*I*n 1857, William H. Gwynn built Gwynn Park to replace another house destroyed by fire earlier that year. Located near Brandywine, in the far south of the county, Gwynn Park possesses a most ornate cornice of molded brick, characterized by historian James C. Wilfong, Jr., as "sophisticated work of the highest order." Historic American Buildings Survey photograph; courtesy of the Library of Congress, Prints and Photographs Division

In 1858 E. G. W. Hall transformed one of Upper Marlboro's early brick homes into this fine residence of the Italianate style. Long known as the Buck House (for its last private owner, Harry Buck), it was restored to its colonial appearance and rechristened Darnall's Chance in 1988 (page 253). The house is publicly owned. Historic American Buildings Survey photograph; courtesy of the Library of Congress, Prints and Photographs Division

This is a rare photograph of the Prince George's County courthouse which stood from 1801 to 1881. It was on that parcel of land that is now between Pratt and Main streets, northeast of the present courthouse. This was the second courthouse in Upper Marlboro; it replaced the frame structure built when the county seat was moved from Charles Town in 1721. Courtesy of Lansdale G. Sasscer, Jr.

Charles Benedict Calvert (1808-1864), the second son of George and Rosalie Calvert, inherited the Riversdale plantation near Bladensburg. He was an agriculturalist as well as a practical farmer, serving as president of the Prince George's and Maryland Agricultural Societies and as vice-president of the United States Agricultural Society. Elected to Congress in 1861, he led the fight for the creation of the United States Department of Agriculture. This photo was taken by Mathew Brady during the Civil War. Courtesy of the Library of Congress, Prints and Photographs Division

Charles Benedict Calvert's scientific farming techniques were the subject of many articles in the agricultural journals of the day. Unlike most Prince George's planters, Calvert did not grow tobacco. He raised grains, hay, and vegetables and practiced animal husbandry. Frederick Law Olmsted included an account of a visit to Riversdale in his book, *A Journey in the Seaboard Slave States* (1856). This is Cinderella, Charles Benedict Calvert's prize Durham cow, as she appeared in the July 1845 issue of *The American Farmer*. Her pedigree was traced back to England; she was born on April 20, 1838. Courtesy of the Prince George's County Historical Society

Friend of both George and Charles Benedict Calvert, Henry Clay visited Riversdale regularly. A bedroom was reserved for his use; there he wrote much of the speech proposing the Great Compromise of 1850. The Calverts cared for him in his final illness. Perhaps no other house outside of Washington has been the home of so many congressmen. Among the twentieth-century residents of Riversdale have been Senator Hiram Johnson of California, Senators Thaddeus and Hattie Caraway of Arkansas, and Representative Abraham Lafferty of Oregon. Since 1949 it has been the property of the Maryland-National Capital Park and Planning Commission. Courtesy of the Library of Congress, Prints and Photographs Division

*A*dvertisements of slave escapes appeared frequently in the newspapers from colonial times right up to the Civil War. Slave violence against masters was extremely rare here, and running away was the most dramatic form of resistance to the slave system a master usually encountered. This advertisement appeared in *The Planters' Advocate,* an Upper Marlboro newspaper, on November 16, 1859. The Forest of Prince George's County was the name given a large, heavily forested area on the east side of the county. Its boundaries were never precisely defined, but its northern limit was around Glenn Dale, and it extended south almost to Upper Marlboro. Courtesy of the Hall of Records, Annapolis

$500 Reward.

RANAWAY from the subscriber, living near the Brick Church, in the Forest of Prince George's County, Maryland, on Tuesday, the 16th of September, 1856, negro man BEN, commonly called

BENJAMIN DUCKETT.

I purchased him from Mr. Edmund B. Duvall. His father and mother belongs to Mr. Marcus Du Val, near Buena Vista Post Office, in this county; and he, no doubt, may be found in that neighborhood.

BEN is of a dark ginger color, about twenty-five years of age, five feet ten or eleven inches high; has an impediment in his speech, and when spoken to has a down look and pats his left foot. His clothing not recollected, as he has various kinds.

I will give the above reward for his apprehension—no matter where taken—provided he is brought home or secured in jail, so that I get him again.

ZACHARIAH BERRY of Washington.
November 10, 1858—tf

A slave coffle is depicted passing the United States Capitol, in the days before the rotunda was built. In contrast to Prince George's County, slaveholding actually declined in the District of Columbia throughout the antebellum period. By the time of the Civil War, there were far more free blacks in the city than slaves. This engraving appeared in *Popular History of the United States,* by William Cullen Bryant and Sydney Howard Gay (1880). Courtesy of the Library of Congress, Prints and Photographs Division

*M*ost slaves lived in small, rude cabins. J. Harry Shannon, the *Washington Star's* first "Rambler," visited Prince George's County in 1906 and identified this structure as the old Hatton slave quarters. He was incorrect. This was an abandoned farm building in the community of Chapel Hill, near Piscataway, when black families converted it into residences in the latter part of the nineteenth century. Courtesy of the Columbia Historical Society

Chapter 6

CIVIL WAR

The Civil War began in Maryland on April 19, 1861, one week after the firing on Fort Sumter, South Carolina. The Northern states responded enthusiastically to President Lincoln's call for 75,000 volunteers to suppress the Southern rebellion, and troops began pouring into Washington. Many of them passed through Baltimore. Pro-Southern Baltimoreans were outraged, and the outrage turned to violence. When soldiers of the Sixth Massachusetts Regiment tried to march from one Baltimore railroad station to the other (to complete their connection to Washington), rioting broke out, and soon there was fighting between the troops and the mob. Even when the regiment made its way out of the city, the lawlessness and rioting continued. The police could do nothing, and neither could the militia.

The violence subsided within several days, but worried federal officials in Washington watched Maryland with concern. If Maryland went out of the Union, the city of Washington—the federal capital—would be surrounded by Confederate states. Although there was strong Unionist sentiment in Maryland—particularly among the farmers of Western Maryland and the business community in Baltimore—the government in Washington decided it could take no chances. President Lincoln authorized the suspension of the writ of *habeas corpus*. Gen. Benjamin F. Butler occupied Annapolis, seized the railroad between that city and Washington, and then on May 14, in a thunderstorm, occupied Baltimore. Maryland was saved for the Union, whether it liked it or not.

In Prince George's County, there was great sympathy for the South. It is not hard to understand why. Despite the sectional division within Maryland, Prince George's County in 1861 *was* part of the South. It had a plantation economy and a population that was more than half slave. There was virtually no abolitionist sentiment here—in the presidential election of 1860, Abraham Lincoln received just one vote from all of Prince George's County! The leaders of our social and public life—the old gentry—were all slaveholders and very much Southern-oriented. When it became evident that Maryland would not secede from the Union, scores of young men went South to fight for the Confederacy.

This sympathy for the South did not necessarily mean that Prince Georgeans wanted Maryland to secede, however. Prince George's was a conservative place, and secession was a radical step. Furthermore, county citizens could be sure, located so close to Washington, that their county would be turned into a battleground if Maryland did try to secede. There were firebrands in the county who advocated secession, but three times they were defeated at the polls by more moderate forces. The sentiment of the voters seemed to be: let the South go in peace, but we will stay in the Union.

The first test of secessionist sentiment in the county took place in February 1861, before Fort Sumter. All across the South, state conventions were being held to decide the question of secession or union. Such a convention was to be held in Maryland, and Prince George's County was to elect four delegates. But instead of sending the delegates, Prince Georgeans voted—by a narrow margin—against holding the convention at all. *The Planters' Advocate* complained that "the least exertion on the part of the friends of the movement, could have elicited a vote that would have overwhelmed the opposition," but the complaint was too late. The state convention, when it met in March, did not decide for secession anyway.

The second electoral test came in June, in special congressional elections. There were two candidates seeking to represent this district in Congress: Charles Benedict Calvert of Riversdale and Benjamin Gwinn Harris of Saint Mary's County. Calvert, though a slaveholder, was a Unionist. Harris was the nominee of the Southern Rights Convention. Calvert carried the county as well as the entire district and went to Congress. His credo was brief: "If Maryland has grievances under the general government she should seek a remedy for them in and not out of the Union." *(National Intelligencer)*. He denied that any state had the right to secede.

The third and final contest of 1861 was in the fall, with the general election for state and county offices. Two slates were presented to the voters of Prince George's County—a Unionist slate and a Peace and States' Rights slate. The Unionist ticket was led by its state senate candidate, Dr. John H. Bayne, the respected physician from Oxon Hill, and a slaveholder. The Peace and States' Rights ticket was led by Oden Bowie, an equally respected planter from Collington. The Unionists were victorious at the polls. Again, *The Planters' Advocate* complained that "Numerous rumors of intended [military] interference, not only prevented a full turnout of the people, but, we have no doubt, affected the course of many who did vote." The total vote was off some from the previous general election, but not dramatically. Whether "rumors of interference" could make people change their votes is debatable.

More than 120 years after the war, it may be hard to understand why Prince Georgeans, on the one hand, sympathized with the South, but on the other hand, voted for the Union for themselves. The entire issue hinged on the question of the preservation of slavery as an institution. As long as slavery was not threatened, Prince George's County would not move to secede. In the first critical year of the war, it must be remembered, the government in Washington made it clear that Maryland and other border states could keep their slaves if they would remain in the Union. The war against the South, in 1861, was a war against rebellion, not slavery. Furthermore, Unionist candidates in this county were not Republicans (there were none here then), but slaveholders themselves, often from the county's oldest families. Finally, Prince Georgeans would not have to fight against the South if they did not want to. There was no draft in the first year of the war, and even after one was begun, substitutes could be found elsewhere in the state to go in the draftee's place. But above all, as long as there could be both Union and slavery, the collective preference of Prince Georgeans, as expressed at the polls, was to stay in the Union.

When the war began, Washington was an undefended city. Many of the troops called up in the first months of the war did not go off to fight, but rather stayed in and around Washington and Maryland to protect the capital. There were soldiers all up and down the Baltimore and Ohio rail line to Baltimore, the rail link to the North; at Fort Washington on the Potomac; in camps throughout the District of Columbia, as well as Bladensburg; and in a ring of forts hastily built surrounding the city. Most of these new forts, such as Fort Dupont, were within the District of Columbia, but one, Fort Lincoln, was partially in Prince George's County, and another, Fort Foote, was entirely in the county, high above the Potomac on Rozier's Bluff, opposite Alexandria.

The Union soldiers who came to Washington often recorded their impressions of Prince George's County. Despite the votes for Unionism, the county had a pro-Southern reputation because of its slave system and lack of enthusiasm for the war. Warren Handel Cudworth, who wrote the *History of the First Massachusetts Infantry* (1866), recorded his thoughts on a march through the county early in the war: "The march [from Bladensburg] commenced . . . and continued, without opposition, through a semi-hostile country until night, when the soldiers bivouacked in an oak-grove, not far from the quaint old town of Marlborough. . . . The people were moderately disunion or non-committal in their sentiments, but emphatically desirous . . . to be left alone. No arms or uniforms were found among them, although several houses were searched from cellar to attic, and the regiment moved on." The people of Bladensburg had been more to his liking: "Most of its inhabitants were loyal to the Union, although not so outspoken, on account of threats and insults from secessionists, as they would have been in New England."

As the war dragged on and became bloodier and bloodier, though, the sentiment of the citizenry here swung away from Unionism toward fuller support of the South. By then, however, the question of Maryland's secession was no longer a live one. The fatal blow to the cause of Unionism in this county came when the Lincoln administration finally linked the winning of the war with the freeing of the slaves. The county Unionists protested that "as Union men, we are not only opposed to emancipation in this state, but even to all agitation of the question, [even though] our devotion to the Union increases with its perils." (*Baltimore American,* September 3, 1863). But their protests were to no avail. They were beaten handily in the local elections of 1863, and a government openly hostile to President Lincoln and the war effort was installed in Upper Marlboro.

What of the blacks in Prince George's County during the Civil War? When slavery was abolished in the District of Columbia in April 1862, a good many fled there to freedom. If the complaints of county officials are a good gauge, the slaveholders saw it as a major problem. Many slaves also escaped bondage by enlisting in the Union Army. Charles Branch Clark, in an article in the *Maryland Historical Magazine* in 1946, reported that Oden Bowie lost seventy slaves to enlistment in 1863. Ironically the Emancipation Proclamation did not free the rest of the slaves here, as it applied only to states in rebellion — and Maryland had not seceded. A new state constitution — passed narrowly by the Maryland voters (but rejected in Prince George's County) — eventually freed the Maryland slaves on January 1, 1865. The old plantation system, already in disarray because of the war and so many runaway slaves, received its death blow.

There were no battles in Prince George's County during the Civil War, although the Union Army was always present, guarding the rail line, marching through the countryside, and watching from the forts around Washington. Once, however, a sizeable Confederate force entered Prince George's. It happened in July 1864, during Jubal Early's last Confederate invasion of Maryland. Early dispatched four hundred cavalrymen under the command of a Marylander, Gen. Bradley Tyler Johnson, to cut rail communications north of Baltimore and then between Baltimore and Washington. The Confederates did their work here on July 11, blowing up the rail line at Beltsville and cutting the telegraph wires. They then camped for the night at the Maryland Agricultural College (now the University of Maryland). The Rossborough Inn was turned over to General Johnson for use as a headquarters. A legend persists that a ball was held at the college that night, a

ball attended by all the Confederate officers, the college faculty, and the pro-Southern gentry of Prince George's County. It may never be known whether there is any truth behind the legend of the "Old South Ball," but the story was repeated time and time again in the decades after the war. The next day Johnson and his men rejoined the main body of Early's forces for the unsuccessful attack on Fort Stevens. Georgia Avenue passes by the old fort now; the battle there was the only one to take place within the District of Columbia.

This history of the Civil War in Prince George's County will end with the story of the hero of the Southern cause here, Walter (Wat) Bowie. Wat Bowie was an officer in the Confederate Army, a captain in Mosby's Rangers. His father was W.W.W. Bowie, the agriculturalist; his mother was Adeline Snowden Bowie. During the war, Bowie returned to the county several times, both to gather information and to visit his family. Effie Gwynn Bowie writes in *Across the Years in Prince George's County* that the federal government put a price on his head. He was captured once and imprisoned, but escaped before he could be executed. Mrs. Bowie relates another story; that while visiting relatives once, he escaped capture by disguising himself as a slave woman and brazenly walking past Union soldiers searching the property. His luck ran out, however, in 1864. On a foray into Maryland, Bowie and his men raided a store in Sandy Spring, Montgomery County. They were pursued by the locals, who caught up with them near Rockville. Shots were fired, and Bowie fell, mortally wounded. His brother Brune stayed with him and was captured. Wat Bowie was buried at the family home, Willow Grove, near Holy Trinity Church, Collington. He was twenty-seven. It is said that his mother never spoke after his death. She died a few months later.

The end of the war and the freeing of the slaves brought great changes to Prince George's County. The old way of life for the slaveholders came to an end; freedom at last came to the slaves. In two hundred years of settlement, Prince George's County had become the richest, most productive plantation county in Maryland. That was over. A new age would begin.

On April 19, 1861, the men of the Sixth Massachusetts Regiment attempted to march through Baltimore on their way to join the defenses of Washington. They were met and harassed by pro-Southern crowds, and fighting broke out. The entire state was aroused; Baltimore was near hysteria. The federal government quickly promised not to send any more troops through the city, and the situation calmed. Federal officials decided, however, that they would have to act to be sure Maryland would not secede. Within weeks the state was occupied by Union troops. Courtesy of the Enoch Pratt Free Library, Baltimore

This was the banner of the Planters Guard, one of the many local military companies that were organized in the tense months before the war broke out. When it became clear that Maryland would not secede from the Union, many of the guard's members went south to fight for the Confederacy. Courtesy of the Prince George's County Historical Society

"TRUTH ALONE IS KNOWLEDGE—KNOWLEDGE IS POWER"

UPPER MARLBOROUGH, MARYLAND, WEDNESDAY MORNING, NOVEMBER 16, 1859.

The Planters' Advocate, one of two Upper Marlboro newspapers, called for Maryland to secede from the Union. Its column of war news was entitled "Progress of the Second War of Independence." The newspaper was denied the use of the mails late in 1861, effectively putting it out of business. It was reborn a few months later, however, as *The Prince Georgian.* Courtesy of the Hall of Records, Annapolis

*T*roops from the Northern states established many camps in and around the city of Washington in the early months of the war. Camp Casey, near Bladensburg, was one of them. It was located in what is now Cottage City— then farmland, the scene of the Battle of Bladensburg five decades before. This lithograph was prepared by E. Sachse and Company of Baltimore. Courtesy of the Library of Congress, Prints and Photographs Division

*T*his article was in *The Planters' Advocate,* May 29, 1861. Courtesy of the Hall of Records, Annapolis

PROGRESS OF THE SECOND WAR OF INDEPENDENCE.

INVASION OF VIRGINIA.

Occupation of Alexandria----Death of Col. Ellsworth, &c. &c.

Our community was thrown into considerable excitement on Friday last upon the receipt of news that a body of Federal troops, from Washington, had occupied Alexandria and the surrounding country, and that their commander had been slain. The reports of the particulars were various and exaggerated, but the news turned out to be substantially true. Probably the occurrence ought not to have occasioned as much surprise as it did, for this movement has been for a long time expected. It was well known in Virginia that General LEE never contemplated making a stand at Alexandria, and that no efforts have been made at all to fortify or occupy any of the adjacent heights. A defensive operation at Alexandria did not seem to fall within his plan— partly, perhaps, on account of the untenable nature of the place, and partly because of risking a battle where the enemy would be so near to reinforcements at Washington.

The Troops from Washington.

During Thursday night last the preparations for the movement were completed in Washington, and two bodies of troops started on the expedition—the Michigan regiment and some other forces by way of the Long Bridge, and Col. ELLSWORTH's New York Firemen Zuaves, by water, from their encampment on the Eastern Branch. The latter force was that which has been stationed at the Insane Asylum on this side of the Eastern Branch—having been removed there from the city on account, as was stated, of their disorderly and unruly behavior. The regiment is composed of rowdy New York Firemen. ELLSWORTH, their commander, was the Captain of the Chicago Zuaves, who visited Washington some months ago. He seems to have been a pet of Mr. LINCOLN's, came on with him to Washington, and has been in attendance upon him ever since. He has been mentioned as an aspirant for almost every sort of office. On the declaration of the present Federal War against the South, he be-

A ring of forts was built around Washington to defend the city. Battery Jamison, part of the Fort Lincoln complex, was in Prince George's County; so was Fort Foote on the Potomac River, whose large guns, with those of Fort Washington downstream, protected against attack by river. This undated photo of the ramparts of Fort Foote was taken sometime in the late nineteenth century. Courtesy of the National Archives

During the Civil War, the guns defending Washington pointed out toward Prince George's County. These are troops of the Third Regiment, Massachusetts Heavy Artillery, at Fort Lincoln, overlooking Bladensburg. Courtesy of the Library of Congress, Prints and Photographs Division

Although no major battles took place here, Prince George's County still was considered part of the "seat of war." This panoramic view was published by J. Bachmann of New York in 1861. Prince George's communities on the map are Bladensburg, Beltsville, Good Luck, Long Old Fields (Forestville), Upper Marlboro, and Queen Anne (drawn on the wrong side of the Patuxent River). Fort Washington is also marked. Courtesy of the Library of Congress, Geography and Map Division

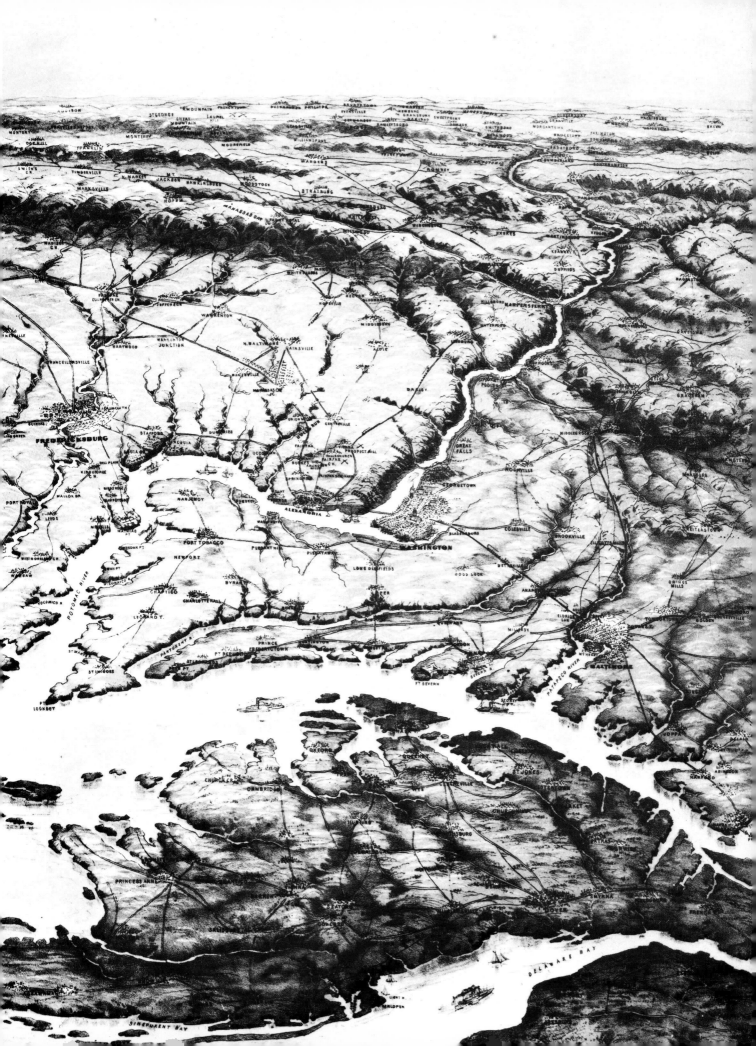

Throughout the war, federal troops guarded the Baltimore and Ohio Railroad line in Prince George's County. The line was Washington's most important rail link to the North. This contemporary sketch by noted Civil War artist Alfred R. Waud depicts the ironworks at Muirkirk, between Beltsville and Laurel. Courtesy of the Maryland-National Capital Park and Planning Commission

These black troops were photographed at Fort Lincoln. Prince George's planters complained that Union soldiers encouraged their slaves to leave their plantations and enlist in the Union Army; some of Prince George's blacks did indeed serve the Union cause. Courtesy of the National Archives

The Old Capitol Prison, on the present site of the Supreme Court Building, was built as a temporary home for the United States Congress after the British burned the Capitol in the War of 1812. During the Civil War it was a prison. George Wilson, editor of the *Marlboro Gazette,* was imprisoned here briefly in 1862 for questioning government draft policies in his newspaper. Wat Bowie was also once imprisoned here, but he escaped. Courtesy of the National Archives

Benjamin Lewis Lanham was one of the many young men from Prince George's County to fight for the Confederacy. He served in the Second Maryland Infantry, one of several regiments of Maryland men. He fell at Gettysburg in the assault on Culp's Hill, just one month shy of his nineteenth birthday. Courtesy of Paul Lanham

"To you need I depict the scene
When next we answered roll?
Are ye surprised that strong men wept,
As home the truth fresh came,
When silence was the sole response
To many a comrade's name?"
　　　　　"Charge of the Second
　　　　　　Maryland Infantry at
　　　　　　Culp's Hill, July 3,
　　　　　　1863—Its Unparalleled
　　　　　　Gallantry," by
　　　　　　William H. Laird

*U*pper Gisboro, a plantation on the south side of the Anacostia River, became an important cavalry depot during the war. It was the home of George Washington Young, descendant of an old Prince George's family. The house was located on the river opposite Fort McNair, in the District of Columbia. Courtesy of the National Archives

PRINCE GEORGE'S COUNTY TICKET

The Union Forever!

For President,
ABRAHAM LINCOLN.

For Vice-President,
ANDREW JOHNSON.

FOR ELECTORS
Of the State of Maryland for President and Vice-President of the United States.

HENRY H. GOLDSBOROUGH
WILLIAM J. ALBERT,
WILLIAM H. W. FARROW
WILLIAM S. REESE
R. STOCKETT MATHEWS
ISAAC NESBITT
GEORGE W. SANDS

For Governor,
THOMAS SWANN

For Lieutenant-Governor,
CHRISTOPHER C. COX

For Comptroller,
ROBERT J. JUMP

For Judge of Court of Appeals—4th **Dist.**
DANIEL WEISEL

For Attorney General,
ALEXANDER RANDALL

For Congress—5th District.
JOHN C. HOLLAND

For Circuit Judge,

For the State Senate,
HENRY N. YOUNG

For House of Delegates,
JOHN HARRIS
JOHN SIMMS

*T*he Union cause had its supporters in Prince George's County even after the Emancipation Proclamation, though their numbers were few. President Lincoln received 197 votes here in 1864; his Democratic opponent received 1,550. Courtesy of the Maryland Historical Society, Baltimore

The actor John Wilkes Booth was the assassin of President Lincoln. Courtesy of the Library of Congress, Prints and Photographs Division

After John Wilkes Booth shot President Lincoln, he fled across the Navy Yard Bridge to Anacostia and then into Prince George's County. This view is from the Washington side, looking over into Anacostia, at Eleventh Street. The photograph was taken sometime in the 1850s. Courtesy of the D.C. Public Library

*T*he only woman implicated in Booth's conspiracy was Mary Surratt of Prince George's County. She owned a tavern in Surrattsville and operated a boardinghouse in Washington. She knew Booth, for he visited her son often in their Washington home. The man who operated her tavern at Surrattsville claimed she aided Booth's escape; she hanged for it. Most today believe she was innocent. Courtesy of the Library of Congress, Prints and Photographs Division

*M*ary Surratt's boardinghouse (left) was in Washington at 604 H Street, N.W. The building still stands, now part of the Chinatown district. Courtesy of the Library of Congress, Prints and Photographs Division

*Th*e tavern at Surrattsville was depicted in *Harper's Weekly.* Mary Surratt visited here the day of the assassination, and John Wilkes Booth stopped here during his flight to Virginia. John M. Lloyd, the tavern keeper, claimed Mrs. Surratt left field glasses for Booth to pick up that evening. Most assassination scholars do not believe him, but the military commission that tried Mrs. Surratt did. The Surratt House is now a museum. It is located on Brandywine Road, near the intersection with Woodyard Road. This is now the heart of Clinton. The community was renamed after the Civil War. Courtesy of the Library of Congress, Prints and Photographs Division

Chapter 7

OLD PRINCE GEORGE'S COUNTY

With the end of the Civil War, Prince George's County entered into a new era. The Civil War accomplished a social and economic revolution by freeing the slaves, and no longer could the old plantation system be sustained. The land was still there, but it meant nothing without the labor to work it. So the old plantations were slowly broken up, and a new age began: an age of small farms, quiet country villages, and modest living. This was the Prince George's County our fathers and grandfathers knew; this was the age we call "Old Prince George's County."

First let us examine the economic consequences of emancipation and the war. Agricultural statistics compiled by the United States Census Bureau tell the story. In 1860 Prince George's County produced more than thirteen million pounds of tobacco; in 1870 it produced not quite four million. Wheat production was similarly affected: 313,000 bushels were produced in 1860 compared to 78,000 bushels in 1870. Corn production was off, too. It decreased from 700,000 bushels in 1860 to 518,000 ten years later. Even the livestock population declined, and the number of acres of improved farmland dropped from 182,000 to 125,000. The wealth Prince George's County knew before the Civil War simply vanished. A rich county had become a poor one.

As dramatic as these statistics might be, though, they do not convey the sense of loss and defeat felt by those who had prospered in the old society. Their letters and their writings do that better than any numbers can. "Since 1865 there had been a demoralizing upheaval in all conditions of life," wrote Effie Gwynn Bowie in *Across the Years in Prince George's County.* "Gentlemen had henceforth more to do than ride over their estates as Lords of the Manor . . . and ladies [were] obligated to . . . accustom themselves to a round of duties unthinkable before." Mrs. Bowie's father, a Confederate officer who was wounded twice during the war, returned to Prince George's County to find "his home burned, his slaves dispersed, and his patrimony scattered." Captain Andrew Jackson Gwynn, C.S.A., went to work as a traveling salesman for a New York importing house. In his daughter's words, "The enchanted spell was broken."

For the black community of Prince George's County, however, the new era was not one of lost fortunes and dashed dreams; it was an era of glorious freedom. "O how fervently they did praise the Lord for their deliverance from slavery!" wrote Nellie Arnold Plummer in a memoir of her family she entitled *Out of the Depths, or the Triumph of the Cross.* She was born a slave herself, the youngest daughter of Adam Francis Plummer of Riversdale and Emily Saunders of Three Sisters, a Hilleary plantation near Lanham. Her parents met at Riversdale in 1839, while Emily was there visiting a sick relative. They were married two years later, but save for infrequent visits, were forced to live apart until emancipation finally freed them. Adam Francis Plummer saw his wife move twice: first from Three Sisters to Meridian Hill in Washington, and then from Meridian Hill to Howard County. He saw her on the auction block at Three Sisters, with their newborn baby in her arms; who can imagine the heartbreak he suffered years later when he learned that his oldest daughter was being sold South, to New Orleans? The entire family was eventually united at Riversdale after the war. "Although I was only six years old, I shall never forget the light and glow that radiated from Mother's cheeks,"wrote Miss Plummer some sixty years later. "Had our Black Folk the education, I think they would have written Psalms that would have far excelled . . . the Psalms of David." For the Plummers, emancipation was neither a political nor an economic act; it was a humane act that freed them from the curse of slavery.

Adam Francis Plummer and his family stayed in Prince George's County, and they eventually became the owners of a small farm near Hyattsville they called Mount Rose. Most of the newly freed slaves became farmers, although few of them, at first, could afford to buy land of their own. Instead, they worked as laborers, tenant farmers, or sharecroppers on the old plantations. The Freedmen's Bureau was active in Prince George's County right after the war, assisting the blacks in beginning lives in freedom, insuring that they truly were freed. Many blacks, understandably, left the county upon gaining freedom: by 1870, 30 percent of the black population was gone. Quite a few eventually returned, however, for by 1880 their numbers were almost back to the prewar levels. These new citizens — almost half of the population — settled into lives as farmers and farm workers. They built churches, schools, and societies of every kind. From the depths of slavery they built an active community life in old Prince George's County.

After the turmoil of the Civil War and immediate postwar years, the leaders of the state began to try to revive agricultural production by encouraging immigration and investment in the old slave regions. In 1867 the state senate published a report promoting the same and describing Prince George's County lands as "safe and valuable investments, better by far than anything that can be obtained in western or northwestern lands." The availability of county farmland was advertised throughout the country, even in the West. Such promotion continued through the succeeding decades. The report of the Maryland Land Office for 1889-1890 hailed Prince Georgeans as people "of a social and friendly disposition, and ever ready to welcome the stranger seeking a home amongst them." "The great want is an honest, industrious immigration," the report concluded. "There is plenty of room for immigrants."

Immigrants did indeed come to Prince George's County. They bought land here, parts of the old plantations, and they helped develop a new agricultural system, a system of small farms. The white population of the county almost doubled between 1860 and 1900, from 10,000 to 18,000. The number of farms increased from 800 in 1870 to 2,400 in 1900, while the average farm size decreased year by year: 159 acres in 1880, 142 acres in 1890, 111 acres in 1900. Agricultural production improved substantially over the 1870 levels under the new system; by 1880 Prince George's farmers were producing six million pounds of tobacco annually. Tobacco would remain our most important crop, although truck farming would become important in this era, too, particularly in the northern portions of the county.

Who were the new immigrants who helped bring prosperity back to Prince George's County in the late nineteenth century? They were, principally, farmers from other parts of the state and nation who were drawn here by the opportunity to buy good land at good prices. There were a few new settlers, though, who built homes along the railroad lines, and instead of farming, rode the trains into Washington to government jobs. In the nineteenth century, though, their numbers were still small - the age of the suburbanite was yet to come.

Perhaps of greater interest to the long-established residents of Prince George's County were the Germans who came here as the nineteenth century entered its final years. Although they did not come here in large numbers, there were enough of them to support a German language Lutheran church in Bowie (Trinity, now First, founded in 1910); establish the Southern Maryland German-American Bank in 1912 (later the Bank of Brandywine); and give the land new place-names such as Silesia and New Glatz (in the Potomac River regions). Perhaps the large German populations in Washington and Baltimore first attracted these foreigners to this region; they were, in any case, the first European group to come to this county in any number since the British settlers of the colonial period.

As the population grew, so did the county's school system. Maryland's modern system of public education was created by the School Act of 1865; it mandated the establishment of public school systems in all of the counties. Dr. John H. Bayne was the first president of the Prince George's County school board, and the task that faced him was formidable: to transform a decentralized system of district free schools — poorly attended — into a strong, well-attended, county system. First he had to convince the wealthy and middle-class farmers — the "opulent classes," as he called them — to forsake the many private schools they had established across the countryside and send their children to the public schools. His strategy was simple: "In proportion as we elevate the standard of education, will our new system be patronized." He was proved right. The private schools closed as the public schools gained public acceptance. In 1865 there were 43 primary schools here. By 1885 there were 69, and by 1908, 112 — 73 white and 39 black. The county's first high school was opened in Laurel in 1899. The schools were, of course, strictly segregated by race, and remained so until the 1960s.

The politics of old Prince George's County was intensely partisan and quite competitive throughout the late nineteenth and early twentieth centuries. During the sixty-year period between 1870 and 1930, the Democrats and Republicans were of equal strength, and each party regularly turned the other out of office. Often the voters sent bipartisan county governments to Upper Marlboro. How, we may ask, did this come about?

At the end of the Civil War, the Democratic Party was stonger than any party has ever been in this county. In the late 1860s, its candidates won elections here by margins of nine and ten to one. There were few white voters willing to champion the party of Lincoln, emancipation, and Reconstruction. But then in 1870 the situation suddenly changed: the Fifteenth Amendment to the United States Constitution was adopted, and black men were given the right to vote. There was no question which party they would support, and overnight the local Republican Party became competitive. In 1871, with solid black support at the polls, the Republicans managed to elect one county commissioner (Lewis Magruder of Landover). In 1872 they carried the county for President Grant. Then, under the leadership of Col. Samuel Taylor Suit, the Republicans swept to victory in the county elections of 1873. Colonel Suit (for whom Suitland was named) was elected to the state senate, and every other office (with the exception of clerk of the court) fell to the GOP.

During the course of the next sixty years, the two parties would take turns governing and sometimes share power. They were so evenly balanced that a shift of just several hundred votes could throw an election from one side to the other. Now that the Republicans were competitive, many whites who at first shunned the party joined it. One Republican county commissioner of the late nineteenth century was Dr. John L. Waring of Nottingham—a Confederate veteran! Other representatives of the old slaveholding families also found a political home in the party of Lincoln. The minority of whites who called themselves Republicans, together with the black voters of the county, made the local GOP very powerful indeed and insured a strong and vigorous two-party system. Throughout this period, there was a continual rotation in county offices. Political careers were short; no one went to Upper Marlboro and stayed there for ten or twenty years.

The Prince George's County of old—the agricultural county, the county of small farms and country villages—is now a memory. Suburban development has changed the face of much of our county; even in the rural districts the automobile has changed the pace of life. In 1880 a Washington journalist named George Alfred Townsend wrote a poem about old Prince George's County. There are no words that evoke the mood and spirit of old Prince George's better than his:

Upper Marlb'ro'

*Through a narrow, ravelled valley, wearing down
    the farmer's soil,
The Patuxent flows inconstant, with a hue of clay
    and oil,
From the terraces of mill-dams and the temperate
    slopes of wheat,
To the bottoms of tobacco, watched by many a
    planter's seat.*

*There the blackened drying-houses show the
    hanging shocks of green,
Smoking through the lifted shutters, sunning in the
    nicotine;
And around old steamboat-landings loiter mules
    and overseers,
With the hogsheads of tobacco rolled together on the
    piers.*

*Inland from the river stranded in a cove between the
    hills,
Lies old Marlb'ro' Court and village, acclimated to
    her chills;
And the white mists nightly rising from the swamps
    that trench her round,
Seem the sheeted ghosts of memories buried in that
    ancient ground.*

*Here in days when still Prince George's of the
    province was the queen,
Great old judges ruled the gentry, gathering to the
    courthouse green;
When the Ogles and the Tayloes matched their Arab
    steeds to race,
Judge Duval adjourned the sessions, Luther Martin
    quit his case.*

Here young Roger Taney lingered, while the horn
  and hounds were loud,
To behold the pompous Pinkney scattering learning
  to the crowd;
And old men great Wirt remembered, while their
  minds he strove to win,
As a little German urchin drumming at his father's
  inn.

When the ocean barks could moor them in the
  shadow of the town
Ere the channels filled and mouldered with the rich
  soil wafted down—
Here the Irish trader, Carroll, brought the bride of
  Darnall Hall,
And their Jesuit son was Bishop of the New World
  over all.

Here the troopers of Prince George's, with their
  horse-tail helmets, won
Praise from valiant Eager Howard and from
  General Wilkinson;
And (the village doctor seeking from the British to
  restore)
Key, the poet, wrote his anthem in the light of
  Baltimore.

One by one the homes colonial disappear in Time's
  decrees,
Though the apple orchards linger and the lanes of
  cherrytrees;
E'en the Woodyard mansion kindles when the
  chimneybeam consumes,
And the tolerant Northern farmer ploughs around
  old Romish tombs.

By the high white gravelled turnpike trails the
  sunken, copse-grown route,
Where the troops of Ross and Cockburn marched to
  victory, and about,
Halting twice at Upper Marlb'ro', where 'tis still
  tradition's brag,
That 'twas Barney got the victory though the British
  got the swag.

But the Capital, rebuilded, counts 'mid towns
  rebellious this—
Standing in the old slave region 'twixt it and
  Annapolis;
And the cannons their embrasures on the Anacostia
  forts
Open tow'rd old ruined Marlb'ro' and the dead
  Patuxent ports.

Still from Washington some traveller, tempted by the
  easy grades,
Through the Long Old Fields continues cantering in
  the evening shades,
Till he hears the frogs and crickets serenading
  something lost,
In the aguey mists of Marlb'ro' banked before him
  like a frost.

Then the lights begin to twinkle, and he hears the
  negroes' feet
Dancing in the old storehouses on the sandy business
  street,
And abandoned lawyers' lodges underneath the long
  trees lurk,
Like the vaults around a graveyard where the courthouse is the kirk.

He will see the sallow old men drinking juleps, grave
  and bleared—
But no more their household servants at the courthouse auctioneered;
And the county clerk will prove it by the records on
  his shelves,
That the fathers of the province were no better than
  ourselves.

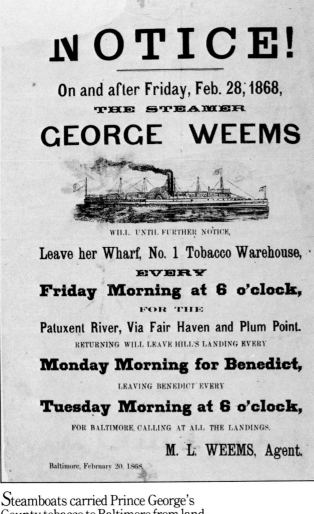

Steamboats carried Prince George's County tobacco to Baltimore from landings on both the Patuxent and Potomac rivers. The *George Weems* was a Weems line steamer, named for the man who founded the line in 1817. Hill's Landing was located in Prince George's County by the present-day Route Four bridge, and served as Upper Marlboro's port on the Patuxent River. Courtesy of the Calvert Marine Museum, Solomons, Maryland

One of the county's leading political figures of the Civil War and post-Civil War era was Oden Bowie (1826-1894), governor of Maryland from 1869 to 1872. A veteran of the Mexican War, he served in both houses of the state legislature and ran unsuccessfully for lieutenant governor before his election to the governorship. He was instrumental in the reorganization of the state's Democratic party after the Civil War. His plantation Fairview (located near Collington), is still a working farm. Governor Bowie was a railroad man as well as a planter and politician; he was president of both the Baltimore and Potomac Railroad and the Baltimore City Passenger Railway Company. The old town of Bowie, at the junction of the two branches of the Baltimore and Potomac Railroad, was named for him. Governor Bowie also raised thoroughbred horses and was president of the Maryland Jockey Club. Effie Gwynn Bowie, in *Across the Years in Prince George's County*, recalled a reception at Fairview, her first visit there as a young schoolgirl: "I recall that I was much impressed with the flow of champagne and the platters of trussed partridges, looking like miniature turkeys. The Governor was a dignified and typical Southern Maryland host and one of Prince George's most public-spirited and distinguished citizens." Courtesy of Oden Bowie

*T*he only resident peer in the American colonies was Thomas, Lord Fairfax, who settled in Virginia in 1747. The title descended through several generations of the Fairfax family in Britain and America until 1869, when it passed to John Contee Fairfax, M.D., of Prince George's County (pictured here). The son of Albert Fairfax and Caroline Eliza (Snowden) Fairfax, Dr. Fairfax chose to remain here with his medical practice. His son, Albert Kirby Fairfax, moved to England early in this century and was confirmed in his title by the House of Lords in 1908. The latter's grandson Nicholas, the fourteenth and current Baron Fairfax of Cameron, has many relatives in Prince George's County. This likeness of Dr. Fairfax appeared in a memoir of his cousin, Richard Snowden Andrews, edited by Tunstall Smith and published in 1910. It was made from a daguerrotype taken about 1855. Courtesy of the Prince George's County Historical Society

*N*orthampton was the home of Dr. John Contee Fairfax near Largo. Built by the Spriggs early in the eighteenth century, Northampton was the seat of a vast plantation in the central part of the county. It was the home of the patriot Osborn Sprigg and later of Governor Samuel Sprigg. Dr. Fairfax purchased the property during the Civil War. The house burned down in 1909. Extensive archeological investigations of the plantation's slave quarters were undertaken during the 1990s. An interpretive site there is now open to the public. Courtesy of the Library of Congress, Prints and Photographs Division

him until the expiration of that time, but he will probably be brought on here in a few days to remain in jail until the day designated by the Governor for his execution.

The Ratification Meeting.

The colored citizens held their Fifteenth Amendment ratification meeting on the plantation of Clement Hill, Esq., near this village, on Monday last, which was numerously attended by their own people, of either sex, and many gentlemen of the vicinity. The officers and speakers comprised about an equal number of white and colored, and the utmost decorum and good order was preserved throughout the day, both in our town and upon the grounds. Some of the speakers were decidedly temperate in their remarks, a Mr. Hawkins, colored, of Baltimore, especially devoting himself to the task of encouraging his race to habits of industry, honesty and temperence, which, if adopted, can but render them useful and prosperous citizens. After the speeches and the reading of letters of declension from prominent Republicans who had been invited to be present, the meeting adopted a series of congratulatory resolutions, and adjourned. The line was then formed and the procession marched back to town, where, about 7 o'clock, they dispersed and returned to their homes. Hays' Brass Band from Washington discoursed fine music during the afternoon, and serenaded some of our citizens at night.

A similar meeting was held in Nottingham on Tuesday, which passed off very quietly and harmoniously, we understand.

Sale of Fine Stock, &c.

S. T. Suit, Esq., of this county, lately sold his thorough-bred three-year old "Bill Wilber," by Planet, out of a Senater mare, to Sheridan Shook, of New York, for $5,000.

case, the "GREAT HENDERSON COUNTY, KENTUCKY, PRIZE SCHEME," has powerful attractions for even the most staid. Here are great fortunes, to be won without haggard toil, and the whole secured by a legal charter, and in the hands of men of the most undouted integrity. We are ready to aid any of our friends who may command us, in securing tickets or information about this matter.

Bladensburg Election.

An election for Town Commissioners in Bladensburg took place on Monday last, the 6th instant, and resulted in the choice of the Citizens' Ticket. The following is the vote received by the respective candidates:

CITIZENS' TICKET:

Harrison Wallis..........57 Geo. W. Goldenstroth..52
Charles A. Wells........54 Charles Parker..........45
Charles O. Lewis........53

REPUBLICAN TICKET, (nominated.)

E. P. Godman ....39 Andrew Lowe..........27
Andrew Foulke..........34 Wm. Becket, colored...31
C. H. Lawrence........32

The Citizens' Ticket was composed of four Democrats and one Republican, and the Republican Ticket of four white and one colored man. Twenty-five colored men voted.

Koskoo.

This medicine is rapidly gaining the confidence of the people, and the numerous testimonials of its virtues, given by practitioners of medicine, leaves no doubt that it is a safe and reliable remedy for IMPURITY OF THE BLOOD, LIVER DISEASE, &c.

The last Medical Journal contains an article from Prof. R. S. NEWTON, M. D., President of the Eastern Medical College, City of New York, that speaks in high terms of its curative properties, and gives a special recommendation of Koskoo to the practitioners of medicine. This is, we believe, the first instance where such medicines have been officially endorsed by the Faculty of

In 1870, black men were granted the right to vote with passage of the Fifteenth Amendment to the U.S. Constitution. A local rally in support of the amendment was reported in the *Prince Georgian* of June 10, 1870. The same issue of that Upper Marlboro newspaper reported the results of town elections in Bladensburg, elections in which a black man was a candidate for office. It was the first time a black is known to have run for office in Maryland. William Becket, the black candidate, was once a slave of the Calvert family of Riversdale. He was released from slavery before the Civil War. Very few blacks followed Becket in seeking public office until the post-World War II era. Courtesy of the Hall of Records, Annapolis

HUNTINGTON CITY.

JUNCTION CENTRE of the BALTIMORE & POTOMAC R.R.

MARYLAND.

1870

(30x38½)

COMPILED AND DRAWN BY J.C. LANG.

The second railroad in Prince George's County was the Baltimore and Potomac, built in the 1870s. (The Baltimore and Ohio was the first, in the 1830s.) The company was formed well before the Civil War by planters who wished to establish a rail connection between Southern Maryland and the city of Baltimore, but the project languished for lack of financing. After the war, the Pennsylvania Railroad, seeking a route into Washington, built the road the planters wished—from Baltimore to Upper Marlboro and on to Pope's Creek (Charles County) on the Potomac River. They also built a branch line into Washington for themselves. At the junction of the two, in north central Prince George's County, promoters hoped to build a great city named Huntington; what developed, instead, was a small town named Bowie. This drawing is from a plat of the proposed Huntington City. A number of other small towns and villages grew up along the two Baltimore and Potomac lines in Prince George's County; Brandywine on the Pope's Creek line; and Landover, Lanham, Seabrook, and Glenn Dale on the Washington branch. That Washington branch now carries Amtrak passenger trains in and out of the nation's capital several times a day. Courtesy of the Library of Congress, Geography and Map Division

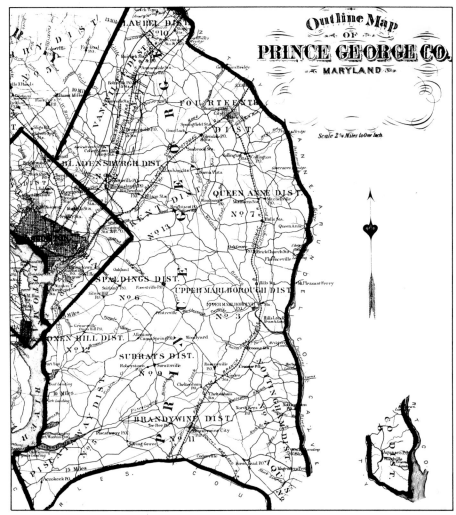

*P*rince George's County was depicted in an 1878 atlas by G. M. Hopkins. Most of the District of Columbia was still rural countryside, and most of the "towns" and post offices in Prince George's County were mere country crossroads. The entire Hopkins atlas, with detailed maps of each election district in the county, was reprinted by the Prince George's County Historical Society in 1975. Courtesy of the Prince George's County Historical Society

*T*he building of fine homes did not end with the Civil War, although the days of the great plantation mansions were over. This is Villa de Sales, also known as the Forbes House, one of the finest of our late-nineteenth-century houses. Built in the Victorian Gothic style for John Dominic Bowling about 1870, Villa de Sales is located near Aquasco. After more than a hundred years, most of the interior and exterior ornamentation is intact. A few years later, Bowling built a slightly smaller twin of this house outside Upper Marlboro. That house, known as Bowling Heights, is on Old Crain Highway at the entrance to Marlboro Meadows. Courtesy of the Maryland-National Capital Park and Planning Commission, History Division

*I*n 1884 Belva Ann Lockwood, a lawyer in Washington, was nominated for president of the United States by women's rights advocates. She opened her campaign for the presidency at Landover, then known as Wilson's Station. Reporters and Lockwood's followers rode out to Wilson's Station on the train and attended a rally at the county home of Amanda Best, one of her supporters. When the evening was over they marched in torchlight procession back down to the railroad stop.

Mrs. Best's home was located at what is now the corner of Landover Road and Seventy-fifth Avenue. A funeral home presently occupies the site. A small log house that once stood on the property—perhaps utilized during the course of the rally—was moved in 1983 to Glenn Dale and placed on a lot in the Camelot community, adjacent to the old home, Maple Shade. Covered with clapboard, as it was then, it has been restored and is used as a residence. Courtesy of the Library of Congress, Prints and Photographs Division

*C*harles Edward Coffin (1841-1912) was a Republican leader in Prince George's County during the late nineteenth century. A native of Boston, he came to this county during the Civil War to manage the ironworks at Muirkirk, which were established in 1847. He later became their owner, a leading manufacturer of charcoal pig iron. In 1883 Coffin was elected to the Maryland House of Delegates, in 1889 to the Maryland Senate, and in 1894 to the United States Congress. With the solid support of the black community, the Republican party was quite powerful in Prince George's County during the late nineteenth and early twentieth centuries. Quite a few Republicans were elected to county office in those years; in several elections the Democrats were completely shut out. Courtesy of the Enoch Pratt Free Library, Baltimore

One of the prettiest churches in Prince George's County is Saint Ignatius Roman Catholic Church on Brinkley Road in Oxon Hill. Consecrated in 1891, it replaced an earlier, simpler structure built in 1849. The tower is eighty feet high, and the interior, save for the altar, has been little changed over the years. Brinkley Road has escaped the commercialization of so many of the other local roads; the church still enjoys a pleasant country setting. Courtesy of Margaret McNeill

This is a detail of Saint Ignatius Catholic Church, Oxon Hill. Courtesy of the Maryland-National Capital Park and Planning Commission, History Division

*T*oday River View is the name of an attractive community along the Potomac River; in days past it was the name of a popular amusement park at Hatton Point. Washingtonians took the steamboat to River View, and one of the thrills that awaited them was this roller coaster, pictured about 1895. River View was one of several parks that flourished along the Potomac River; it closed about 1918. Its dancing pavilion was made into a home, now one of the finest in the River View community. Courtesy of Frederick Tilp

*I*n 1891, the popular steamer *W. W. Corcoran* was beached at Notley Hall after a fire. Courtesy of Frederick Tilp

*B*orn a slave, Joseph Fleet was a seventy-seven-year-old widower when he posed for this photo in 1897. He lived with his son James and his family, who were then tenant farmers at Maple Shade, a Bowie and Addison family farm near Glenn Dale. Ellen (Bowie) Addison was then mistress of Maple Shade; her fine old home still stands as part of the Camelot community. Courtesy of William B. Addison and Mr. and Mrs. Dino Bakeris

*T*his relic of colonial Prince George's County—built sometime in the mid-eighteenth century—stood very close to the Washington Monument until its destruction in 1894. This was once the home of David Burnes, a planter who owned considerable acreage in what is now downtown Washington. Burnes was a justice of the peace for Prince George's County and a man noted for his quick temper. He was not anxious to have the capital city built on his land and clashed frequently with the commissioners planning the city, though he was the first to sell them land needed for public buildings. His daughter married John Peter Van Ness of New York. Next to her father's old home they built a fine mansion designed by Latrobe. The site of the David Burnes house is now occupied by the Pan American Union. Courtesy of the Columbia Historical Society

The corner of Main and Elm streets in Upper Marlboro is shown at the turn of the century, looking toward the courthouse. The oxen and hay wagons are gone now; so is the Bank of Southern Maryland. From *A History of Upper Marlboro* by James H. Shreve (1971)

This was the county courthouse in Upper Marlboro at the turn of the century. Built in 1881 and designed by Frank E. Davis of Baltimore, its Victorian ornamentation was much admired in its day. In 1940 the Victorian facade was hidden by an addition with a portico and massive columns; other additions have completely surrounded the Victorian core. Courtesy of Saint Thomas Episcopal Church, Croom; from the collection of James H. Shreve

*T*he Maryland Agricultural College at College Park was established in 1856 to offer a practical and scientific education for the sons of Maryland farmers. Charles Benedict Calvert of Prince George's County led the movement to create the college, and it was built on a portion of Riversdale, his family estate. Calvert died in 1864, and, deprived of its guiding force, the institution developed slowly. In its first forty years there were fewer than 100 graduates, although many more did obtain some schooling there. All students received military training. This company of cadets assembled on the college hill in 1898. Behind them are the new Chemistry and Mechanical Engineering Buildings, now replaced by Tydings and Taliaferro halls of the University of Maryland. Courtesy of the University of Maryland Libraries, Special Collections Division

*U*ntil several new buildings were added in the 1890s, this building, known as the Barracks, served as the combined dormitory, library, classroom, and administration building for the Maryland Agricultural College. It stood on the hill near the present site of the Shoemaker Building. Built in 1859 by Charles Benedict Calvert, it was destroyed by fire in 1912. Courtesy of the Prince George's County Historical Society

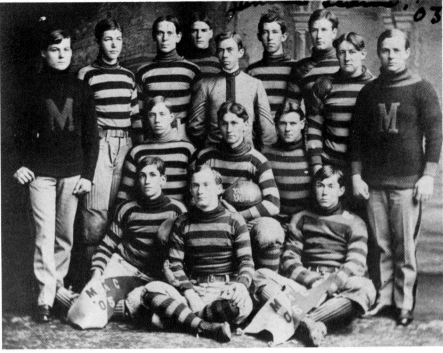

*T*his was one of the early football teams of the Maryland Agricultural College. Courtesy of the University of Maryland Libraries, Special Collections Division

*T*hese ruins were the result of a fire at the Maryland Agricultural College. During the evening of November 29, 1912—while the students and faculty were entertaining their guests at the Thanksgiving ball—a fire broke out that eventually consumed both the new administration building and the old Barracks—the two most important buildings on campus. Overnight the college lost half of its classroom and office space as well as every dormitory room. The Thanksgiving fire proved to be the turning point in the college's history. The college was rebuilt, but its direction changed. The educational program was broadened, women were admitted, and a strong liberal arts program was established. The transformation was completed in 1920 when the old agricultural college became a state university, the University of Maryland, by act of the legislature. Courtesy of the University of Maryland Libraries, Special Collections Division

*F*ort Washington was the scene of artillery tests in the 1890s. This photo was taken on June 29, 1899. Courtesy of the National Archives

*T*he first high school in Prince George's County was built in Laurel in 1899, financed in large measure by the subscriptions of the local citizens. Many additions have been made to the building over the years; it is now the Edward Phelps Community Center, named for the mayor who led the campaign for the school and who actually built it. Other public high schools soon followed: Surrattsville in 1906; Marlboro in 1908 (converting the old academy); and Baden, Brandywine, and Hyattsville in the next decade. The first two black high schools, Marlboro and Lakeland, were opened in the 1920s. Photo by Robert H. Sadler, Jr., about 1904; courtesy of Dr. Robert S. McCeney and John C. Brennan

A young driver waits outside the store at Brightseat. One of the county's largest shopping centers—Landover Mall—now is the trading center at the old Brightseat crossroads. J. Harry Shannon photo; courtesy of the Columbia Historical Society

*T*his was Casey's blacksmith shop in Bladensburg. Courtesy of the Prince George's County Historical Society

The interior of an unidentified black-smith's shop in Laurel was photographed in the 1920s for the Pictorial Archives of Early American Architecture. Courtesy of the Library of Congress, Prints and Photographs Division

The steamboat *Potomac* is shown on the upper Patuxent, about 1900. The view is from the north. Prince George's County is on the right, Anne Arundel County on the left. This is probably the Bristol landing, on the Anne Arundel side, about a mile and a half south of Wayson's Corner and the Route Four bridge. Reprinted from a publication entitled *Baltimore, Chesapeake and Atlantic Railway Company/Maryland, Delaware and Virginia Railway Company (1911).* By then, the railroads owned the steamboat lines. Courtesy of the Calvert Marine Museum, Solomons, Maryland

The Chesapeake Beach Railway, which ran from Seat Pleasant (at the District of Columbia line) to the Chesapeake Bay, passed near Upper Marlboro. Colorado railroad man Otto Mears built the line in the 1890s to convey vacationers from Washington to his resort at Chesapeake Beach; it also served as Upper Marlboro's rail link to the nation's capital. The line was abandoned in 1935. The Upper Marlboro station was built about 1900. It stood on Croom Station Road until vandals burned it down in 1962. Courtesy of the Chesapeake Beach Railway Museum

*I*n this social call at the turn of the
century, Mrs. Geneva (Lanham) Beckett
is at right; the other woman is unidentified. This photo was taken at one of the
farms that became part of the city of
New Carrollton. The house was located
on what is now the 8100 block of Pow-
hatan Street. Courtesy of Paul Lanham

This was Water Street—now Baltimore Avenue—in Bladensburg, about 1893. The George Washington House is hidden by the trees on the left (further up the street) and Hyattsville is beyond. Courtesy of Joseph Shepperd Rogers

The old Palo Alto Hotel in Bladensburg dated from colonial times and stood on Baltimore Avenue across from the George Washington House. During the early nineteenth century visitors to the cockfights nearby adjourned to this bar; tradition holds that it was here that the cocktail was named. In later years, the Palo Alto offered the last chance for a thirsty traveler to partake of a cold beer before proceeding on to dry Hyattsville. Courtesy of Francis X. Geary

*O*ld Bladensburg even boasted an ice cream parlor, where a boy could get a cone on a hot summer day. Courtesy of the D.C. Public Library

*T*his is an early photograph of the Magruder House in Bladensburg, built by William Hilleary in the early 1740s. In a recent restoration, its rafters—all but one or two—were found to be in perfect shape–testimony to the strength and quality of the wood cut from the virgin forests of eighteenth-century Prince George's County. Several physicians have lived in this house, and George Washington dined here on May 9, 1787. The house has been covered with stucco for a long time, for even in the oldest photographs it appears so. The house is known as the Magruder House for Dr. Archibald Magruder and his family, who lived here for many years in the nineteenth century. It is now the home of an accounting firm and stands on Annapolis Road beside the Kenilworth Avenue overpass. Courtesy of Francis X. Geary

*T*he mineral waters of the Spa Spring once drew visitors to Bladensburg, for they were renowned for their beneficial and curative powers. Surrounding the spring was a park, scene of many picnics and political gatherings throughout the nineteenth century. The spring was located at the north end of Water Street (Baltimore Boulevard), now an industrial area. Courtesy of the Prince George's County Historical Society

*U*ntil industrial development swallowed up most of old Bladensburg in the 1940s and 1950s, it was a town of old wooden houses and tree-lined streets. This house, known as Old Clements, was the last pre-Revolutionary frame structure in town. It was built about 1760. Named for onetime owner Thomas Clements, it stood on Forty-sixth Street amidst warehouses and industrial yards, one block north of Annapolis Road. Its massive chimneys and steeply-pitched roof added some character to a street lined with flat-topped industrial buildings. This photograph dates from the early years of the twentieth century. Old Clements burned to the ground in 1985. Courtesy of William A. Aleshire

*A*cross the wooden fences of Bladensburg could be seen the Ross House, a fine brick home built by Dr. David Ross in the 1740s. The house was dismantled brick by brick in 1957 and rebuilt in Baltimore County five years later. The original doors, windows, dormers, trim, flooring, paneling, and even handmade nails were carefully preserved and used in the rebuilding. The Ross House stood on the north side of Annapolis Road, opposite the present entrance to the marina. It was also known as the Old Brick Hospital, for tradition holds that the British put it to such use during the Battle of Bladensburg. Courtesy of Joseph Shepperd Rogers

The ox was a beast of burden in old Prince George's County, and the oxcart was a frequent sight on county roads even in the early years of this century. This group appears to be ready for play rather than work. The photograph was taken by Bruce Davis, who recorded many scenes in southern Prince George's County early in this century. Courtesy of Elmer Trueman and Sandra Cross

This is a family scene in old Prince George's County, about 1904. Three generations of the Perrie family are gathered at the home of J. Benson Perrie (1831-1905) in Westwood, a farming community in the southeastern part of the county. Westwood, today, is still a farming area, as is much of southern Prince George's County. Perrie and his wife Martha are seated at the left; a servant holds Lightfoot, Mrs. Perrie's steed. Other family members pictured are Rinaldo Perrie and his wife Imogene (seated), L. Nelson Perrie and his wife Grace (standing), and children Benson (age two) and Preston (age one). Courtesy of the Perrie family and Sandra Cross

163

This 1907 Potomac River scene shows
the John Swift farm at New Glatz.
Courtesy of Frederick Tilp

A young couple enjoys horse and buggy
days in Forestville. Courtesy of Alice
Baker McLaughlin

These workers are cutting tobacco near Upper Marlboro in 1908. Even though the old plantation system died with the Civil War, tobacco remained Prince George's County's most important crop. The exact location of this scene was not recorded; it was identified only as "Sasscer's fields." Courtesy of the National Archives

A farming family near Piscataway was photographed by J. Harry Shannon, the *Washington Star*'s "Rambler," in 1908. Courtesy of the Columbia Historical Society

*F*or as long as anyone can remember there has been a small yet distinct community of people in Southern Maryland who have lived apart from everyone else and claimed descent from the Piscataway Indians. Their history and culture have been studied by sociologists interested in American isolate groups, but no consensus on their precise origin has been established. Many scholars believe they are of mixed Indian, white, and black ancestry, and white society has generally regarded them as nonwhite. Their family names have appeared in the legal records of Charles and Prince George's counties since colonial times, and over the years they have been known as Wesorts, Brandywine people, or Piscataways. Today, many of them are seeking recognition from the federal government as the Piscataway Indian tribe. Early in this century, J. Harry Shannon photographed these Indian children, as he termed them, near Piscataway. Courtesy of the Columbia Historical Society

*A*fter the tobacco was cut, it was taken to the barns where it was hung and air-cured for several months. This photograph of men loading the cut tobacco onto a wagon was taken in 1921, somewhere near Upper Marlboro. After the tobacco was dried and cured, it was tied into hands, packed into hogsheads, and shipped to Baltimore. The loose-leaf auctions at Upper Marlboro—the means of marketing Prince George's County tobacco today—were not instituted until the late 1930s. Courtesy of the National Archives

Laurel, located on the Patuxent River in the northeastern corner of the county, was a place unlike any other in old Prince George's—an industrial town whose wealth came from cotton mills, foundries, and small industries, rather than tobacco. Its population at the turn of the century was about 3,000, large enough to offer urban advantages unknown elsewhere in the county, yet small enough to retain a smalltown feel. Main Street is shown in this 1908 photograph by Robert H. Sadler, Jr. (1875-1963). His camera work has left for us an invaluable photographic record of old Laurel. The three buildings on the left still stand on the best-preserved Main Street in Prince George's County. Courtesy of Dr. Robert S. McCeney and John C. Brennan

The principal industry in Laurel was the Laurel Cotton Mill, which produced Laurel cotton duck and other products. At the turn of the century (when black smoke was a sign of progress, not pollution) 400 persons were employed at the mill, which was powered by the falling waters of the Patuxent River. The mill was closed before World War II, and the buildings were demolished during the 1940s. This drawing appeared in a 1906 promotional booklet issued by the Improvement Association of Laurel, Maryland; it was reprinted recently by the Citizens National Bank. Courtesy of John C. Brennan

Academy of Music, Laurel, Md.

FAULTLESS BRAND NIGHT ROBES.

E. ROSENFELD & CO. 32-36 S. PACA ST. BALTO. MD.

BROADWAY
NEW YORK

*T*he Academy of Music in Laurel was the scene of concerts, lectures, commencements, traveling shows, and dances. Built in 1879, it burned down on April 4, 1917. No other town in the county could boast such a cultural institution. Courtesy of John C. Brennan

*A*bout 100 people were employed at this factory in Laurel, opened in 1891. There the workers—mostly women—earned fifteen to twenty dollars a week sewing together garments on huge, steam- and belt-powered machines. Photo by Robert H. Sadler, Jr.; courtesy of Dr. Robert S. McCeney and John C. Brennan

*M*arion Duckett (with the bowler hat) leads ice skaters near Bladensburg. Courtesy of the Prince George's County Historical Society

*U*pper Marlboro was a center of horse racing as early as colonial days: this is the racetrack grandstand in 1909. The thoroughbreds ran in Upper Marlboro until 1972, when the track was closed in a reorganization of Maryland's racing industry. In 1988, two days of racing a year, with wagering, were restored. The track is now part of the Prince George's Equestrian Center, operated by the county. Courtesy of Joyce Rumburg

Parades were often seen in Laurel, including the annual Emancipation Day parade organized by the town's black community. Crowds from Washington and Baltimore, as well as elsewhere in the county, came to Laurel for the picnics and celebrations associated with the event. This is the 1910 parade. Photo by Robert H. Sadler, Jr.; courtesy of Dr. Robert S. McCeney and John C. Brennan

"A village unknown to most of the people of Washington lies about fifteen miles southward of the city. It is a village that is not so interesting for what it is as for what it was, but really makes quite an appeal to men who have an attachment for the past." This was how J. Harry Shannon, the Rambler, described Piscataway in the *Sunday Star* of November 29, 1914. Once a busy colonial port, it was, by the middle of the nineteenth century, a quiet country village in southern Prince George's County. This was the main street (now Floral Park Road) as Shannon saw it in 1914. The old tavern and store, pictured here, still stands, now covered with synthetic shingle. The oldest portion of the building (against which the man is leaning) dates from the mid-eighteenth century; the larger part (with porch) dates from the early nineteenth. It served as a tavern and store until the early years of the twentieth century. Courtesy of Frederick Tilp and the Columbia Historical Society

In the early days of military aviation, before the creation of the Army Air Corps, the Signal Corps was assigned the responsibility for developing the airplane for military uses. In 1909 the U.S. Army leased 160 acres of land near College Park and there established the Signal Corps Aviation School—now the College Park Airport. College Park thus became the nation's first military airfield. This photograph, taken in 1912, shows the hangars, medical tent, and the team of nurses on duty during each flight. The Signal Corps closed the school in 1913 and the field reverted to civilian use. It is still in operation today, the nation's oldest operating airport. The College Park Airport is owned by the Maryland-National Capital Park and Planning Commission, which has built a museum on the site. It is located along the Baltimore and Ohio Railroad tracks near the College Park Metro station. Courtesy of the College Park Aviation Museum

A hunting party was photographed in Cheltenham on the grounds of the old reform school. Courtesy of Gloria Wyvill Garner

*W*ilbur Wright is shown working on the engine of one of the Wright brothers' airplanes at College Park in 1909. Orville Wright also worked here in the early days, as did Henry H. ("Hap") Arnold, Benjamin D. Foulois, and the helicopter pioneers of the 1920s, Emile and Henry Berliner. In 1918 the Post Office Department made College Park the Washington terminus of the U.S. Airmail Service. The first regularly scheduled airmail flight in American history left College Park for Philadelphia and New York on August 12 of that year. Later years would also see the Goodyear blimp and DC-3s, among other craft, take off and land at College Park. Courtesy of the Prince George's County Historical Society

*T*he campaign for women's suffrage did not pass by Prince George's County. This photograph is believed to have been taken here in the county—perhaps at the House of Reformation at Cheltenham or in Upper Marlboro—during a traveling campaign by the Just Government League of Maryland. This picture was taken circa 1910. Courtesy of Gloria Wyvill Garner

The Ardmore Union Church, built in 1912, was one of several churches built during the late nineteenth and early twentieth centuries that represented religious traditions new to Prince George's County. Before the Civil War, all of the county's churches — and almost all of her citizens — were either Episcopalian, Catholic, Presbyterian, or Methodist. Population growth in both the countryside and the suburban towns changed that, however, as members of other denominations came in sufficient numbers to support churches of their own. The mother church of Ardmore Union was Concordia Lutheran in Washington, D.C., whose minister would often ride out on the Washington, Baltimore, and Annapolis electric railroad to conduct services on Sunday afternoons. In later years the congregation affiliated with the Evangelical and Reformed Church, and later with the United Church of Christ. Unfortunately the old Ardmore church stood in the path of the Beltway and was destroyed in the 1960s. Its successor is Saint Paul United Church of Christ, Seabrook. Courtesy of H. Louise Coomes

This was the interior of the Ardmore Union Church. Courtesy of H. Louise Coomes

*T*hese people are motoring in old Bladensburg. This is Water Street (now Baltimore Avenue), and the handsome brick building is the George Washington House, still standing. Jacob Wirt built the house about 1760. It served as a store during the colonial era, then as a residence, a tavern, and a hotel. It has been known as the George Washington House since the Centennial in 1876. The Prince George's Jaycees saved the house from destruction in the 1970s; since then it has been owned by a charitable trust. The frame structure next to the George Washington House was Jacob Wirt's tavern, known in colonial days as the Indian Queen. It is no longer standing. Jacob Wirt's youngest son was William Wirt, attorney general of the United States from 1817 to 1829. Courtesy of the Prince George's County Historical Society

One of the earliest federal installations in Prince George's County—other than military fortifications—was the Cheltenham Magnetic Observatory of the U.S. Coast and Geodetic Survey. Established in 1901, the observatory remained in operation until 1956, when its work was taken over by the Fredericksburg Magnetic Observatory and Laboratory in Virginia.

In the 1890s, the government began seeking a site in the vicinity of Washington for the observatory. Cheltenham, fourteen miles to the southeast, was found to be free enough of electrical interference for the scientific instruments, yet close enough to the city and to the Pope's Creek railroad for convenience. The small laboratory and office was built entirely of wood, held together with copper nails and wooden pins. The foundations were made of a local marble almost totally free of magnetic properties. This photo appeared in the 1902 annual report of the U.S. Coast and Geodetic Survey. In the background are the buildings of the Maryland House of Reformation, on whose grounds the observatory was built. Courtesy of the Library of Congress

*M*ilitary discipline is demonstrated at the House of Reformation in Cheltenham. This photo was taken early in this century. The House of Reformation was a school, not a prison. The boys were taught trades and worked the school farm; they lived in dormitories rather than prison cells. The administration maintained close ties to the local community, and residents of the area often used the facilities of the institution as a sort of community center. Courtesy of Gloria Wyvill Garner

*B*oys from the House of Reformation mug before the camera. Courtesy of Gloria Wyvill Garner

*T*he House of Reformation and Instruction of Colored Children, now Boys Village of Maryland, was incorporated by the legislature in 1870 and built on 800 acres of land in Cheltenham donated for that purpose by Enoch Pratt of Baltimore. Its first superintendent was General John Watts Horn, a Union veteran of the Civil War and onetime warden of the state penitentiary. He was appalled that youthful offenders were being incarcerated with hardened criminals, and was one of the leaders of the effort to establish an institution where, according to the first annual report, "they would be free from the influence of bad examples, and, under the guidance of those who would cultivate their better nature, become useful men and citizens." Courtesy of the National Archives

The age of the automobile comes to Prince George's County. This is Main Street, Upper Marlboro, sometime early in the twentieth century. The large building is the Marlborough House hotel, no longer with us. Courtesy of the Prince George's County Historical Society

*J. H*arry Shannon photographed these children with their Teddy bear in 1914. The picture appeared in the *Sunday Star* on November 29 of that year in an article about Piscataway. Shannon entitled the photo "A Snapshot by the Roadside." Courtesy of the Columbia Historical Society

*T*he old Walker Mill stood at the eastern end of Walker Mill Road, not far from Ritchie. Pictured here in 1916, it was one of the last water-powered grist mills to operate in Prince George's County. It finally burned down in the 1920s. Charles H. Walker operated the mill for half a century. He acquired the property shortly after the Civil War from the Berrys, of nearby Concord, who had operated a mill there for at least three generations. The exact age of this mill was not known; it was, however, a very old one. Photo by J. Harry Shannon, courtesy of the Columbia Historical Society

*H*yattsville was the home of the scientist James Harris Rogers (1850-1929), who came to Prince George's County as a young man. Rogers was an electrical scientist, holding more than fifty patents in that field. He was a pioneer in the development of undersea and underground wireless telegraphy; his work in that area was of great importance during World War I. The Rogers system of undersea telegraphy enabled American ships and submarines to communicate with one another and with shore stations without detection by the Germans (who had no such capability); his underground receiving stations could also (without suspicion) intercept regular German wireless messages, a development of great value. Rogers was awarded the inventors' medal by the Maryland Academy of Sciences, who also nominated him for the Nobel Prize. Rogers came to this area in 1877, when he was appointed chief electrician of the United States Capitol, a post he held for six years. He eventually located in this county, in Hyattsville. Courtesy of Joseph Shepperd Rogers

*F*irwood, the home of James Harris Rogers, once stood on Rhode Island Avenue in Hyattsville, where the County Service Building is now located. His laboratory was adjacent to his house. Other members of the Rogers family also settled in Prince George's County in the late nineteenth century. James Webb Rogers, the scientist's father, purchased the Parthenon, an old colonial home in Bladensburg (once a Lowndes and Bowie residence) in 1884; his brothers and sisters also moved here. Courtesy of the Prince George's County Historical Society

This is part of the parade on Main Street, Upper Marlboro, welcoming home Prince George's County's veterans of World War I, October 7, 1919. Among the other ceremonies that day was the dedication of a memorial to those from this county who died in the war, a memorial still on the courthouse lawn. The list of those who made the supreme sacrifice includes several names long associated with this county (Magruder, Sprigg, Edelen, and Baden, among others), but also many new names, reflecting the growth the county was beginning to experience, particularly in the areas adjacent to the District of Columbia. Courtesy of Gloria Wyvill Garner

The women of the Red Cross were part of the parade in Upper Marlboro. The building on the right is the Magruder law office, a Greek Revival structure built before the Civil War by C. C. Magruder, a prominent Upper Marlboro attorney. It served successively as a law office for his son, C. C. Magruder, Jr., and his grandsons, C. C. Magruder III and M. Hampton Magruder. It is still a law office today. Courtesy of Gloria Wyvill Garner

180

While most presidents have visited Prince George's County at one time or another, Dwight Eisenhower was the only president to actually live here. In 1919, while a young army officer stationed at Camp Meade, he and Mrs. Eisenhower lived briefly at Mrs. Ray's rooming house at 327 Montgomery Street, Laurel. This is their wedding picture, taken three years earlier, on July 1, 1916. Courtesy of the Dwight D. Eisenhower Library, Abilene, Kansas

This was the wharf at Trueman's Point, on the Patuxent River, about 1922. Trueman's Point was the southernmost Patuxent landing in Prince George's County, located near the village of Aquasco. During the twenties, two small communities, Cedar Haven and Eagle Harbor, were laid out near Trueman's Point. They were built by black Washingtonians who wished to summer in the countryside. Eagle Harbor is an incorporated municipality, the smallest in this county. Courtesy of H. Graham Wood and Frederick Tilp

The automobile shared the road with the horse and buggy and pedestrians when this photograph was taken. This is Route One at the University of Maryland. Courtesy of the National Archives

The Potomac was once famous for its sturgeon and other fisheries, and there were once hatcheries and commercial fishing operations along Prince George's Potomac shore. The great era of Potomac sturgeon fishing was between 1870 and 1920, when the commercial catch averaged 75,000 pounds yearly. Sturgeon were most sought for their roe, and Potomac caviar was prized in New York and Philadelphia. This photo was taken in 1928. Few sturgeon are seen in the Potomac any more. Courtesy of Frederick Tilp

On October 27, 1927, a barricade was removed from Priests' Bridge, crossing the Patuxent River at Whitemarsh (Bowie), and an automobile parade led by Governor Albert C. Ritchie proceeded to Upper Marlboro. The occasion was the formal opening of the Robert Crain Highway, the first continuous concrete road linking Baltimore and Southern Maryland. The road, fifteen feet wide, was hailed for its commercial as well as its social benefits, and was named for Robert Crain of Charles County, its major proponent before the legislature. Five years earlier, this monument was erected in Upper Marlboro to commemorate the beginning of the road's construction. A bypass now takes the road (U.S. Route 301) around Upper Marlboro, but the monument still stands at the west end of Main Street. Courtesy of the Enoch Pratt Free Library, Baltimore

In 1908 the state of Maryland assumed control of the Baltimore Colored Normal School, a private institution for the training of black teachers, and moved it to Prince George's County, near the old town of Bowie; thus was established Bowie Normal School, an institution which later became a state teachers' college and now is Bowie State University. In this photograph, from the 1920s, a women's tennis class practices in front of the old classroom building. A major building program accompanied the strengthening of the educational program in the 1960s and 1970s, transforming the teachers' college into a modern liberal arts institution. Courtesy of Bowie State University, Thurgood Marshall Library

At her grandmother's house in Broad Creek, Agnes Bertha Cadell posed beside Owen Taylor's automobile, about 1927. Courtesy of Phyllis Luskey Cox

This is a 1928 view of Billingsley, on the Patuxent River, one of the oldest homes in Prince George's County. It probably was standing at the time the county was erected. It was built in the 1690s by Colonel Thomas Hollyday, first chief justice of the county court, and its brick walls are nearly two feet thick. Billingsley was the home of the Weems family between 1740 and 1841; since then it has been owned by a number of Prince George's families. The Meloys held it most of the twentieth century; it is now owned by the State of Maryland. Central peaked dormers were added to each side in the 1930s, as was a wing on the visible gable end. In this picture, Anna I. Meloy and her son Ralph Edward Meloy stand before the house. Courtesy of Mr. and Mrs. Samuel W. H. Meloy

This old church, photographed in the 1930s, is Saint John's at Broad Creek, one of the oldest Episcopal churches in the county. There has been a church at Broad Creek since at least 1695; this one was built in 1766, incorporating part of an earlier church built in 1722. The parish which Saint John's serves was one of the thirty original Anglican parishes of Maryland, created in 1692 when the Church of England was established in Maryland. The church is at the center of the Broad Creek Historic District. Historic American Buildings Survey photograph; courtesy of the Library of Congress, Prints and Photographs Division

These men are judging hands of tobacco at the Prince George's County fair, Upper Marlboro, 1929. Courtesy of the Enoch Pratt Free Library, Baltimore

Horse racing has been popular in this county since colonial times, when gentlemen organized races at Upper Marlboro, Queen Anne, Bladensburg, Piscataway, and other early towns. A packed grandstand watches this thoroughbred race at Bowie racetrack about 1930. Bowie was opened in 1914 and closed seventy-one years later. The last day of racing was July 13, 1985. Horses still run at Bowie, however; it is now a training center. Courtesy of the Enoch Pratt Free Library, Baltimore

*Th*ese travelers were photographed
crossing the Patuxent River on the Chesapeake Beach Railway, on their way to
that famous bayside resort. The crossing
was at Mount Calvert. Courtesy of the
Chesapeake Beach Railway Museum

Chapter
8

THE STREETCAR SUBURBS

THE SUBURBAN IDEAL

To have a roof over one's head and that of his family, to sit by his own vine and fig tree, and to feel that he has his own threshold and hearthstone, is recognized by those experienced in the battle of life... as one of the very first importance. As salaries and wages now are...it is nearly impossible for the man of moderate income who has a family, to purchase or build a house in large cities. Therefore it has become a system in Boston and New York especially, for such persons to live in suburban towns where lots for building purposes may be cheaply procured, and the construction of small houses or cottages advantageously carried on.

So began a promotional tract circulated around the city of Washington in 1868 announcing the availability of building lots at a place called Spa City, near the Spa Spring, "adjoining the village or town of Bladensburg." Spa City is an important place in the history of Prince George's County, important not for what it became (for it never was built), but for what it represented. Spa City was the first attempt to build a residential suburban town in Prince George's County, and the first attempt to induce Washingtonians to make their homes here, even while working in the city. By any conventional measure Spa City was a failure, but the idea behind it was not. Within a few years, other entrepreneurs would begin subdividing other land in Prince George's County, and the county's first suburban towns would be born.

The suburbs of Prince George's County came to be because the city of Washington—a town of just 61,000 in 1860—became a boom-town in the years after the Civil War. The population of the city nearly doubled in the 1860s; it grew by a third in both the 1870s and 1880s. There were hundreds of new federal employees, many with families, and they needed places to live. But the city itself was an expensive place. The Washington *Sunday Chronicle* of August 21,

1881, complained that it was "strange that the capitalists and moneyed men of Washington seeking good opportunities for investment never think of building blocks of small houses within the reach of poor men and government clerks." But in the boom-town economy of postwar Washington, close-in city property was too valuable to use for blocks of small houses. So those small houses were built further out, beyond the city's old legal boundary of Florida Avenue (in what was then the rural countryside of Washington County, D.C.) and across the Anacostia River. After building a fringe of suburban subdivisions around the old city—suburbs like Uniontown, LeDroit Park, and Mount Pleasant—the developers began moving out the railroad lines and extending the system of street railways. None of the street railways yet came to Prince George's County, but the railroad did—the Baltimore and Ohio, through the northern part of the county. Along that line, in the 1870s, 1880s and 1890s, the building of Prince George's County's suburbs began—homes principally for men and women of modest means, who either could not afford city housing prices or who preferred (in the words of another promotional tract) a home "away from the dust and unwholesome clamor of city life, in the quiet and peace of beautiful scenery, and the green fields, fresh air, and religious surroundings of nature." Inexpensive and wholesome living: that was the suburban ideal Washingtonians were promised in Prince George's County.

THE RAILROAD SUBURBS

The Baltimore and Ohio Railroad was built through northern Prince George's County in 1835; it was forty years old in the 1870s. Even before the suburbs were dreamt of, there were small country villages along the line—Bladensburg, Hyattsville, and Beltsville—with schools, churches, and stores already established. That is one of the reasons our first suburban developments were built along that line, rather than along the new Baltimore and Potomac (Pennsylvania) line. The early promotional tracts boasted of the preexisting amenities of the older villages and assured Washingtonians that they were not moving out to the rural wilderness.

Christopher Clarke Hyatt, merchant and postmaster at Hyattsville, was our first successful suburban developer. He and Benjamin F. Guy subdivided the land around the Hyattsville railroad station in the 1870s, and there grew up our first suburban town. Most of the new Hyattsville was east of the railroad tracks, along the present-day Baltimore Avenue, between the Northeast Branch and the railroad crossing. That area is mainly commercial and industrial today, but a few of the early cottages that Benjamin F. Guy built still stand there, representatives of our first suburban housing.

Hyattsville grew rapidly in the late nineteenth century, from a few houses in 1870 to a population of about 1,200 in 1900. The rural country village became a modern little town. On the west side of the railroad tracks a business section—a downtown about two blocks long—was built up, with drygoods and grocery stores, wood and coal dealers, realtors, barbers, and druggists, and quite a few other enterprises, including a building association (important for the growth of a suburban town), banks, and even a newspaper (the *Hyattsville Independent,* founded 1899). On the hills behind this business section, as well as on the east side of the railroad tracks, new homes were erected, some of them grand Victorians that survive to this day. Some of these new houses were summer homes for Washingtonians, but more were year-round residences for commuters and local businessmen. Hyattsville became the focus of our late nineteenth century suburban development. Even after other towns were built up and down the line, Hyattsville remained the preeminent suburb, the business and banking center of the suburban corridor.

As the years went by, other speculators, entrepreneurs, and developers tried their hand at suburban subdivision with varying degrees of success and failure. In 1887 the Calvert family sold 475 acres of the great Riversdale estate (including the mansion) to real estate developers; two years later the land was surveyed and renamed Riverdale Park, and lots were offered for sale. So began the town of Riverdale. Further up the railroad line, near the Maryland Agricultural College, College Park was started in the 1890s, and beyond it Berwyn and Berwyn Heights. Older places like Bladensburg, Beltsville, and even Laurel (fifteen miles from the city of Washington) gained new, Washington-oriented residents. The railroad, in that age before the automobile, was their lifeline. It took them to work in the morning and brought them home at night.

The railroad suburbs brought several hundred—perhaps as many as 2,000—new residents to Prince George's County during the 1880s and 1890s. The "upper line" of Prince George's County—so called even before the suburbs were built—became a thriving little suburban corridor, with new businesses, new schools, new clubs, new churches, and even organized community activities like baseball teams. Despite this growth, though, the railroad towns were *small* towns, remote outposts of the city in a vast rural countryside. No one for a minute yet thought of Prince George's County as a suburban county; the vast majority of our people still derived their livelihoods from agriculture. Right about the turn of the century, however, that would begin to change.

THE STREETCAR SUBURBS

The year 1897 is important in our history because that is when the streetcar came to Prince George's County. After some hard economic times in the early 1890s, the national economy was back on track, and Washington was again growing. The demand for affordable housing was high. The Prince George's County suburbs, with their inexpensive land and low tax rates, were particularly attractive to middle and working class newcomers, but the railroad was not the most convenient means of commuting. Real estate men and railway men both knew that a streetcar line, built for and catering to commuters, would encourage suburban growth. The conditions were right, and so the streetcar came to Prince George's County.

On March 3, 1897, the Maryland and Washington Railway began service from New York and Florida avenues to the District of Columbia line, at what is now Mount Rainier. By 1899 its successor, the City and Suburban Railway, had extended the line on both ends, to the Department of the Treasury building in Washington and to Hyattsville and Riverdale in Prince George's County. By 1902 streetcar service went all the way to Laurel, following closely the course of the Baltimore and Ohio Railroad. The railroad suburbs became streetcar suburbs, and a building boom began.

Hyattsville and the smaller suburban towns grew mightily with the introduction of the streetcar. New suburbs were built along the line, too: Mount Rainier, Brentwood, and Cottage City, among others. The suburban corridor became the county's most densely populated section, the home of several thousand people. But the pressures for affordable housing were still great, and soon suburban growth would spread elsewhere.

The second major suburban concentration in Prince George's County was to develop at the eastern corner of the District of Columbia. In 1900 the Columbia Railway built a streetcar line to the very corner of the district, where it met the Chesapeake Beach Railway. This streetcar line was known as the Bennings line, for it crossed the Anacostia River at the village of Bennings and ran past the old racetrack of the same name. The purpose of the Bennings line

was mainly to service the summer excursion traffic, but it also opened a new section of Prince George's County to suburban development. Within a few years (once winter service was guaranteed) the suburban towns of Seat Pleasant and Capitol Heights were a-building there. Other smaller subdivisions followed. A short branch of the Bennings line was extended to a place called Kenilworth, and there the town of Fairmount Heights—a suburb built by blacks—was begun.

There was some suburban development along two other rail lines in this county, too, but at a much slower pace. Along the Baltimore and Potomac Railroad, Lanham and Seabrook became the homes of several hundred people by the turn of the century; Ardwick became a little commuting village; and old Bowie (Huntington) reported a population of 460 to the 1900 census. These places (and others along the line), though, retained a rural character the towns of the suburban corridor lost. Many of their homes were summer homes, and there was by no means as much business development.

The other rail line through Prince George's County at the time was the Washington, Baltimore, and Annapolis Railway, an electric interurban line that began through-service between Baltimore and Washington in 1908. This electric railway left Washington at Seat Pleasant and headed straight for Baltimore on a course parallel (but a mile away from) the Baltimore and Potomac Railroad. The villages of Lincoln, Glenarden, Ardmore, Dodge Park, and Columbia Park grew up along this line, but they were small places. There was really little local traffic on the Washington, Baltimore and Annapolis Railway; most of its riders were travelers from one city to the other. Though the line itself is long gone, a reminder still exists: the old humpback bridge built to carry Annapolis Road (Defense Highway) over the railway. It now carries Route 450 over the abandoned roadbed.

The only other area of any early suburban concentration in Prince George's County was Takoma Park. Primarily a District of Columbia and Montgomery County suburb, Takoma Park grew up along the Metropolitan Branch of the Baltimore and Ohio. A small portion of the town was built in Prince

George's County, however; that was in our far northwestern corner. The other areas of the county remained largely untouched by suburbanization until the automobile came along. The areas south of the District line—now the heavily developed neighborhoods of Oxon Hill, Temple Hills, Suitland, Forestville, Camp Springs, Clinton, and Fort Washington—saw some increase in population, but they basically remained rural communities until World War II or after. Today, after several decades of intense development there, it may be hard for newcomers to visualize them as farming communities—but they were.

The growth of Washington and the federal government during and after World War I accelerated the pace of suburban development in Prince George's County, particularly along the upper line and at the end of the Bennings line. On May 15, 1927, the *Sunday Star* published a long article examining the rapid change going on in Prince George's County. Entitled "Prince George's, a County of Rural Charm Fringed by Growing Suburbs," the article summarized the history of the county's suburban development. "Prince George's County is most populous along the line of the Baltimore-Washington Boulevard [Route One]. Nearly 15,000 persons [in a county of 60,000] dwell in the narrow, fourteen-mile stretch between Laurel and Bladensburg. This population is essentially suburban. More than 75 percent of it is employed in the government departments and stores of Washington. It represents the national capital's earliest movement beyond the limits of the District of Columbia—which began in the nineties and gained its greatest impetus during the congested days of the World War."

The article pointed out that all this growth was not without its problems. Thomas R. Henry, the author, wrote: "The school problem of Prince George's County is increasingly difficult. The county wants to give the people who are moving into the Washington suburbs as good educational advantages as they would have in the national capital. But these people represent no taxable industry. The school levy must be entirely on real estate. Consequently, the burden is falling heavily on farm property, and every cent must be conserved."

The funding of the schools was, indeed, a problem presented by the development of the streetcar suburbs; the provision of gas, electric, telephone, and emergency service, the building of a water and sewer system, and the construction of roads were too. These problems were tackled—and solved with varying degrees of success—by the county government, municipal governments, the business community, or by the people themselves. This early suburban experience would prove to be an important experience, for time would soon reveal that the era of the streetcar suburbs was just a prelude to a period of rapid growth that would far outstrip anything seen before. Henry Ford and Franklin D. Roosevelt were setting in motion forces that would change the way of life in Prince George's County forever.

*E*lectric streetcars shared Pennsylvania Avenue not with automobiles, but with horse-drawn vehicles, in this view of Washington, D.C. taken about 1904. On the north side of the avenue, the new Willard Hotel flew its own flag, while the stately tower of the Post Office Building dominated the south side of the street. Washington was a boom town in the 1890s and early 1900s, and these streetcars would lead many of the newcomers to homes in Prince George's County. Courtesy of the District of Columbia Public Library

Washington developers and local land-owners began eyeing Prince George's County for suburban development long before the streetcars ever came. This brochure promoted The Highlands, a city that developers hoped to build along the Baltimore and Ohio Railroad line. The Highlands offered several lot sizes and floor plans, including "a handsome cottage for $1,600, a fine villa residence for $2,300, and a large country residence for $3,000." Terms were 25 percent down, with monthly payments not to exceed fifty dollars. According to the brochure, it took just eight minutes to reach down-town Washington by train. The pro-moters claimed that The Highlands would become the "*ne plus ultra*" of sub-urban places about Washington," but such was not to be the case. The city was never built. The Highlands was ahead of its time; 1870 was too early for such an ambitious project. Cottage City was eventually built in its place, begun by Charles M. Lightbown in 1915—after the streetcar came through. The entire brochure for The Highlands was re-printed in *A History of the Town of Cottage City, Maryland* (1976). Courtesy of the Library of Congress

This was the symbol of suburban growth, the streetcar. These commuters were going home to Takoma Park, about 1910. Courtesy of Catholic University Archives, the Terence V. Powderly Collection

Christopher Clarke Hyatt (1799-1884) was a merchant, postmaster, and founder of Hyattsville. In 1845, Hyatt bought some land about a mile north of Bladensburg, where the old Baltimore-Washington Turnpike (Route One) met the Baltimore and Ohio Railroad line. There he opened a store, and the crossroads became known as Hyattsville. In the 1870s, Hyatt and other landowners began subdividing the surrounding property for house lots; thus was born Prince George's first railroad suburb, a country village for workers in Washingotn. Hyattsville was formally incorporated in 1886; its charter made it a dry town. Courtesy of Francis X. Geary

Hyattsville's railroad station was built in 1884. Designed by E. Francis Baldwin, it replaced a much simpler structure. Although it is long gone, a similar station—built the same year and designed by the same architect—survives in Laurel. Courtesy of Gloria Wyvill Garner

The man most responsible for the development of that part of the suburban corridor closest to Washington was Capt. Wallace A. Bartlett (1844-1908). A native of Warsaw, New York, he came to Washington after the Civil War and became a patent examiner for the federal government and later a patent lawyer in private practice. In 1887 he moved out to the country—to what is now Brentwood, Maryland. With several partners he purchased several hundred acres of land close to the District line. There, in the late 1890s and early years of this century, he began the development of Brentwood, Mount Rainier, and North Brentwood, selling hundreds of small lots to new suburbanites.

Bartlett was a Union veteran. Wounded and captured in the Wilderness Campaign, he served as commander of the Hyattsville post and the Maryland department of the Grand Army of the Republic. He also campaigned for Prohibition and temperance causes and became an influential civic leader in the suburban areas of Prince George's County. Courtesy of the Enoch Pratt Free Library, Baltimore

The homes of the early suburban towns were of many types, from small, simple cottages to large, grand houses. This house was built in Riverdale in 1890, one of the first constructed after the platting of the townsite. Its Queen Anne details are beautiful representations of the craftsmanship of that era. Located on Oliver Street, it was the childhood home of banker and businessman A. H. Smith, Sr. (1903–1987), and remained in the Smith family for one hundred years. There are scores of other fine homes such as this one scattered throughout the old streetcar suburbs of Laurel, Hyattsville, Riverdale, College Park, Berwyn, and Berwyn Heights. Courtesy of the Maryland-National Capital Park and Planning Commission, History Division

This house once stood in old town College Park, at the end of College Avenue near the railroad tracks. In its long life it served as a private residence, an apartment house, and a fraternity and sorority house. The oldest house in town, it was actually older than College Park itself—built shortly after the Civil War for Ella Calvert Campbell, daughter of Charles Benedict Calvert of Riversdale, on her part of her father's estate. She eventually sold this house and the land around it to developers who began building College Park in the 1890s. Many of the town's early residents were faculty members at the Maryland Agricultural College (now the University of Maryland). The Ella Calvert Campbell house was destroyed in the 1960s and replaced by an apartment building. Courtesy of the Prince George's County Historical Society

One of the prominent business and civic leaders of the new suburbs was William Pinkney Magruder (1857-1939). Born into one of those old county families whose fortunes fell with the Civil War, Magruder foresaw the growth of the suburban towns and recognized the business opportunities they represented. He moved to Hyattsville in 1882 and lived there until his death. He bought a lumberyard and later established a hardware company, "thereby facilitating the development his vision foreshadowed" (American Clan Gregor Society yearbook, 1939). He invested in real estate and is said to have become the largest landowner in Prince George's County. Magruder was an officer of several suburban financial institutions, served on the Hyattsville city council and as mayor of that town, represented Prince George's County in the Maryland House of Delegates, and was elected a county commissioner. The land that became Magruder Park was his gift to the city of Hyattsville; he also left a fund for the care of sick children, now administered by Prince George's General Hospital. Courtesy of the Prince George's County Historical Society

198

*D*owntown Hyattsville, Prince George's County's first suburban town, is shown about 1905. Almost 2,000 people lived in Hyattsville then, and many of them worked in Washington. This street was called Maryland Avenue; it is now the 5100 block of Baltimore Avenue (Route One), between Farragut and Gallatin streets. The view is to the north. The tracks in the foreground are the streetcar tracks; their electric wires are strung overhead. From this point Hyattsville's commuters could ride all the way to downtown Washington in a matter of minutes—much faster than we can drive it today. The photographer stood on the railroad tracks to get this picture, back in the days before the grade crossing was closed. Courtesy of the Maryland-National Capital Park and Planning Commission, History Division

*T*he Hyattsville Shaving Parlor was founded in 1893 by Benjamin F. Chinn, who is shown posing in front of the shop. His establishment served the community for five decades. Courtesy of Francis X. Geary

Before a modern sewer system was built, someone had to clean and lime the outhouses. In Hyattsville, Steve Bailey and his mule Maud performed that task faithfully for many years. Hyattsville did eventually build a primitive sewer system that emptied into the branch early in the century. In 1918 the state legislature created the Washington Suburban Sanitary Commission to provide water and sewer service for all of Maryland's Washington suburbs (including those in Montgomery County), but it was decades before all the suburban areas were hooked up. Courtesy of Francis X. Geary

Gas service—for cooking and lighting—came to the suburban towns with the formation of the Hyattsville Gas and Electric Company in 1906. By 1907 there were 210 customers and six miles of mains. A year later the patronage had doubled, and mains stretched all the way to Mount Rainier and Brentwood. The gas was manufactured at this plant in Edmonston, on what is now Tanglewood Drive. The tank is long gone, but the old factory still stands. Courtesy of Francis X. Geary

The home-delivery wagons of Keefauver and McMillan's general store were a familiar sight in the streetcar suburbs before the days of the automobile. The store was located on Berwyn Road in Berwyn, near the streetcar line. Like all of the streetcar suburbs, Berwyn's business district (if one can call it that) was along the railroad and streetcar line. Route One did not become the "main street" of the suburban corridor until the age of the automobile. A number of old commercial buildings like this one can still be found up and down the streetcar right-of-way (now Rhode Island Avenue) in Riverdale, College Park, and Berwyn. Courtesy of the Maryland-National Capital Park and Planning Commission, History Division

*H*orses and livery stables were part of the early suburban scene. This livery stable in Hyattsville was photographed early in the twentieth century. Courtesy of Francis X. Geary

The children of the suburbs posing here in 1907 were gathered for the birthday party of Eugene Bennett (age 9) and Edith DeGroot (age 7) in Riverdale. The *Riverdale Sentinel* of November 28, 1913, reported that there were 126 children enrolled in the Riverdale School for the fall term—79 boys and 47 girls. Riverdale was built on what was once the Calvert estate, Riversdale. The fine old mansion still stands in the center of town. Courtesy of the Riversdale Society

The 4500 block of Burlington Road, Hyattsville, is pictured in 1910. The population boom that came with the streetcar at the turn of the century made mass-produced blocks of housing like this possible. Courtesy of Francis X. Geary

The suburbs were not all white. Fairmount Heights was a black suburb; so were North Brentwood and Lakeland (north of College Park). The older suburbs had black neighborhoods, too; this family lived in East Hyattsville, a small black community later absorbed into Edmonston.

This was the Johnson family about 1910. From left to right, in the back row, are Lucy Johnson, a widow, and her sons Robert and Thomas. Charles, Albert, and Luetta are in front. Robert, twenty-two years old in 1910, worked at the nearby ice plant; Thomas, younger, was then a laborer at odd jobs. The number of whites who came to the suburbs far exceeded that of blacks, and year by year the black percentage in the population declined. Old Prince George's County was once about 50 percent black; by 1960 blacks constituted less than 5 percent of the population. Courtesy of Catholic University Archives, Terence V. Powderly Collection

With war clouds hovering over Europe, America mobilized. Here, in 1913, Company F of the First Infantry, Maryland National Guard, is ready to leave for camp from the Hyattsville train station. Most of the men were from Hyattsville and nearby communities; they became Company F of the 115th U.S. Infantry during World War I. The Meuse-Argonne offensive was but one of the actions they participated in during that war. Courtesy of the Prince George's County Historical Society

This was the end of the line at Laurel. The car is marked "Treasury," and its destination was the Treasury building at Fifteenth and G, next to the White House. Streetcar service was gradually discontinued as the age of the automobile advanced. Service on the main line through the suburban corridor of upper Prince George's County was cut back from Laurel to Beltsville in 1925; to Branchville in 1949, and then finally eliminated in 1958. Robert H. Sadler, Jr., photo; courtesy of Dr. Robert S. McCeney and John C. Brennan

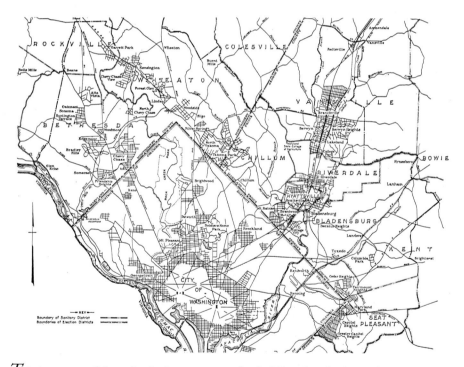

This is a map of the suburbs in 1918, when suburban growth was still tied to rail and streetcar lines. The two major centers of early suburban development in Prince George's County are quite evident: the towns of the suburban corridor in upper Prince George's County and the towns at the corner of the District of Columbia. The automobile has changed this picture completely. Now decades later, almost every bit of this area is filled in with suburban development, not to mention more land to the south. This map was published in the report to the Maryland General Assembly proposing the creation of the Washington Suburban Sanitary Commission. Courtesy of the Prince George's County Historical Society

This is an early view of Seat Pleasant, a town that derives its name from the old colonial land grant of the same name. Seat Pleasant was the center of Prince George's County's second suburban concentration, a series of small towns clustered around the eastern corner of the District, at the end of the Bennings streetcar line. This building was the Farmers and Mechanics Bank; behind it is the Chesapeake Beach Railway station. Streetcars took Seat Pleasant commuters to work until 1949, when the Bennings line was finally closed. Courtesy of the Chesapeake Beach Railway Museum

This picture of Central Avenue through Capitol Heights was taken in December 1924. Capitol Heights was the first of the towns at the corner of the District of Columbia to incorporate, doing so in 1910. Courtesy of Blanche L. Ennis

This was Central Avenue, looking back into the District from Capitol Heights, 1919. There was still much undeveloped land in the District while Prince George's suburbs were being built. The early suburbanites looked across the District line not at the city of Washington, but at rural countryside. Courtesy of Blanche L. Ennis

LINCOLN, MARYLAND,

A SUBURB OF

GREATER WASHINGTON, D. C.

Pleasant Ride from United States Treasury Building via Washington, Baltimore and Annapolis Electric Railway, Passing the Union Station

"The Center of the Nation"

The Lincoln Land and Improvement Co.
Incorporated
2500 Pennsylvania Avenue, S. E.
WASHINGTON, D. C.

WATCH LINCOLN GROW

CAPITOL HEIGHTS, MD.,
Sept. 7, 1910.

MR. ZANTZINGER:

I was renting a small house in the suburbs at a moderate rent, and always paid in advance. I started a store in it. When the agent came for the rent he said: "Oh, you have a store. I will have to raise the rent," and sent me a 30 days' notice to move or pay more rent. I paid the extra rent until I moved in my own home at Capitol Heights. After buying the lots the next thing was to find some one to build. I had some money in the bank, and after a while, about the middle of the winter when the snow was on the ground, I found a carpenter to suit my terms of what I could pay, with my son helping to build my little home. Now we have added more rooms and rent them for a store. How much better it is to own your home. Whatever you have around you is yours. All of us feel very happy by our own fireside. The payments are very easy. I don't think they could have been better. Capitol Heights is very healthy and beautiful, and I like it very well for a good many reasons.

(Signed.)   T. E. EAGEN.

One of the few suburban developments along the Washington, Baltimore, and Annapolis electric railway was Lincoln, a black community laid out soon after the line was opened in 1908. It attracted quite a few black professionals from Washington, both as investors and residents. Lincoln, today, is reached by either the Martin Luther King, Jr., Highway (Route 704) or Annapolis Road (Route 450). It is a community of large lots and tall trees; the passing motorist is probably unaware of the pleasant community that lies not far off the highway. Courtesy of the Library of Congress

This testimonial to the benefits of life in early Capitol Heights was taken from a promotional brochure issued by the town's developer, O. B. Zantzinger, Sr. Courtesy of Blanche L. Ennis

207

This class photo in an unidentified
suburban school was taken about 1925.
Courtesy of the Prince George's County
Board of Education

*T*his pamphlet, published in 1926, unabashedly sang the praises of "the suburban towns of upper Prince George's County." By then, almost 20,000 people lived in the "combined territories," and buses, as well as trolleys and the train, took commuters into Washington. Courtesy of Edith Bagot

*I*n the era before interstate banking, locally-owned financial institutions served the needs of the county's families and businesses. Three such institutions established in the early days of the streetcar suburbs grew to be financial giants in the second half of the twentieth century. Maryland Federal Savings and Loan was founded as the Hyattsville Building Association in 1887; Suburban Bank as Prince George's Bank in 1915; and Citizens Bank of Maryland as Citizens Bank of Riverdale in 1924. Suburban and Citizens no longer exist; they were absorbed by out-of-state banks in 1986 and 1997, respectively. This building, still standing on Route One in Hyattsville, was built for Prince George's Bank as its headquarters in 1926. Courtesy of Francis X. Geary

Chapter 9

FIFTY YEARS OF SUBURBAN GROWTH: 1930-1980

In October 1928, on two successive Sundays, the *Baltimore Sun* published two long articles about Prince George's County. While they took note of the suburban towns growing up along the rail and streetcar lines, the articles still concluded that "Prince George's County is primarily an agricultural county," devoted to the cultivation of tobacco. "This crop is one of the few in which ancient farming methods prevail as successfully as modern machinery," explained the Sun, "and in Prince George's, the patient ox holds unchallenged his place of honor as man's aid in the cultivation of the fragrant weed."

How Prince George's County changed in the next fifty years! The agricultural county became a suburban one, and the family station wagon replaced the patient ox as the symbol of the local lifestyle. Farming did not disappear completely from the county, nor did rural countryside, but in sheer numbers — both economic and demographic — Prince George's County became overwhelmingly suburban in character.

Suburbanization came to Prince George's County in two distinct phases. The first phase was a period of tremendous population growth from 1930 to 1970. The second phase, which began about 1970 and continues to this day, has been characterized more by economic diversification than by population increase. The contrasts between these two phases are stark ones, but together they tell the story of the suburbanization of Prince George's County.

In 1930, the population of Prince George's County was 60,000. By 1970, it was 660,000 — an elevenfold increase. Few counties in the nation have experienced such tremendous growth in such a short period of time; indeed, in the 1960s, Prince George's County was the fastest growing county in the United States. How and why did such growth occur?

The primary reason for the rapid growth of Prince George's County during the period 1930-1970 was the growth of the federal government. It is no coincidence that the county's great population boom began in the same decade as the New Deal. When Franklin D. Roosevelt became president in 1933 there were 63,000 government jobs in Washington; by 1940 there were 166,000. The population of Prince George's County increased by 50 percent in the same decade, from 60,000 to 90,000 residents. The succeeding decades saw even greater population growth; during the 1960s alone the county gained 300,000 new citizens. The homebuilding industries prospered and grew in this era, and so did the providers of local consumer services

— banks, supermarkets, retail stores, and the like. Otherwise, there was little new economic development or diversification. Suburban Prince George's County became a classic bedroom community. Newcomers settled here because they could find work in Washington — either in the public or private sector — and because they could find solid, affordable housing in Prince George's County. They worked in the central city by day and slept in the county by night.

The great population boom of 1930-1970 changed the face of Prince George's County. Over the course of those forty years huge areas of the county became thoroughly suburban. Henry Ford, perhaps, was as responsible for that as the federal government, for his revolution — making the automobile affordable for every family — opened the vast rural regions of Prince George's County to suburban development for the first time. No longer did suburbs have to be concentrated along streetcar lines; they could now spread across the land.

And spread they did. First in the northern areas of the county, near the older, preexisting streetcar suburbs, and then, after World War II, even to the rural districts south of Washington. The opening of the Suitland Federal Center and Andrews Air Force Base in the 1940s encouraged the suburban development of the southern region; so did new bridges across the Anacostia River. Gradually all of the area now described as "inside the Beltway" became filled with housing developments, apartment complexes, and shopping centers. Indeed, when it was built in the early 1960s, the Beltway — Washington's circumfrential highway — defined the boundary between rural and suburban Prince George's County. But suburbanization did not stop at the Beltway; it spread even further, along the highways that led like the spokes of a wheel out into the countryside. Indian Head Highway, Branch Avenue, Central Avenue, Annapolis Road, and Route One all became major corridors of beyond-the-Beltway development during the great population boom. Suburbia set down roots even amidst cornrows and tobacco fields.

All of the counties adjacent to Washington, D.C., experienced rapid suburban development during the four decades after 1930, and in most respects the experience was much the same. Nevertheless, the suburbanization process in Prince George's county had distinctive characteristics of its own, differing in several respects from the process in neighboring jurisdictions.

First and foremost among these was its middle and working class nature. Regional analysts have long debated why neighboring Montgomery County attracted so many more affluent residents than did Prince George's; they have offered reasons ranging from particular zoning laws and governmental structure to the character and foresight of the leadership in the respective counties. In truth, however, the differences between the counties had more to do with residential patterns already established in Washington, D.C., than anything else. During the latter part of the nineteenth century, upscale development flourished in the northwestern sector of the city (adjacent to Montgomery County), while middle and working class communities became the norm in east Washington (adjacent to Prince George's County). Suburbanization of the two Maryland counties simply extended those historic residential patterns.

Another characteristic distinctive to Prince George's County was the growth of a black suburban population. Before suburbanization, blacks lived in all of the counties of the region, in small villages and rural communities that often predated the Civil War. Only in Prince George's, however, did blacks build new suburban towns during the streetcar era; only in Prince George's County did blacks, in any number, move into newly-built residential communities in the 1940s, 1950s and 1960s. These new communities were generally built adjacent to the old black towns of streetcar days, for residential segregation was still the rule. Nevertheless, of all the counties of the region, Prince George's, the old slave county, proved the most hospitable to black suburban aspirations during the boom period. The groundwork was thus laid for a large black in-migration during the 1970s, when fair housing laws opened all of the county to black settlement.

Prince George's County endured the same growing pains as the other counties in the area during the boom period: zoning battles, crowded classrooms, roadbuilding without end, and a continual demand by the citizenry for more government services with no increase in taxes. The furious pace of growth in the sixties and the problems it engendered contributed in no small measure to the voters' decision in 1970 to abandon the longstanding county commissioner form of government and adopt, in its place, a home-rule charter government with an elected county executive and county council. The efforts of civic activists begun more than twenty-five years before bore fruit in 1971 with the inauguration of William W. Gullett, charter activist and former mayor of College Park, as Prince George's first county executive.

The great population boom finally came to an end around 1970. During the next ten years, the county gained only 5,000 more residents — the smallest ten-year increase since the nineteenth century. A number of factors brought the boom to an end: a state-imposed ban on new sewer-line construction in most of the county, which drastically curtailed new home construction; the attraction of cheaper land and lower tax rates in counties beyond Prince George's; "white flight" occasioned by both school busing and the movement of blacks into certain areas near the District; the end of the postwar baby boom, which diminished the rate of natural increase; and a slowdown in the rate of governmental growth itself. For forty years, economic growth in Prince George's County had been dependent on population increase. Without it, could economic prosperity be sustained?

The county's new charter government looked to the example of other suburban jurisdictions in the region. Years before, they had eschewed the role of bedroom suburbs in favor of economic diversification. Somewhat belatedly, but with great determination, Prince George's County followed suit. A new economic development strategy was established in the first charter administration of William W. Gullett (1971-1974). It reached full flower in the "New Quality" program of his successor, Winfield M. Kelly, Jr. (1974-1978), and continued under the administrations of county executives Larry Hogan (1978-1982) and Parris N. Glendening. Under their leadership the county attracted the same kinds of high-tech, marketing, and research and development firms that had so strengthened the economies and the tax bases of its neighbors.

As Prince George's County's economy diversified, skyscraping office buildings rose up at Beltway interchanges and new, landscaped office parks became busy employment centers. By the early 1980s the metropolitan Washington Council of Governments reported that more Prince Georgeans worked in the county than in the District of Columbia, a dramatic reversal of the historic suburban pattern. Prince George's County could rightly claim that it was well on the way to becoming an equal partner in a dynamic regional economy. Fifty years of suburban growth transformed an old tobacco county into a metropolitan one.

This was a scene in Greenbelt, the new Prince George's County, just before World War II. Perhaps no community better symbolizes the changes Prince George's County has experienced during the suburban era than the city of Greenbelt. Built in the 1930s on farm and forest land, it became home to several thousand new Prince Georgeans — natives of Massachusetts, Nebraska, Alabama, Ohio, and other faraway places — most of whom came here to work for the federal government. Even Greenbelt's architecture heralded a new age; the town's principal buildings were designed in the Art Deco style. After more than half a century of service, the city pool still offers relief in the summertime. U.S. Farm Security Administration photo; courtesy of the Libray of Congress, Prints and Photographs Division

Built by the federal government during the Depression, Greenbelt was a New Deal employment project to be sure, but more importantly, an experiment in city and social planning. Greenbelt was one of three "green towns" built by the U.S. Resettlement Administration during the 1930s (the others were in Ohio and Wisconsin). They were planned communities full of trees and parks and free of urban congestion. The privately-built planned communities of Columbia, Maryland, and Reston, Virginia, owe much to Greenbelt and the planning principles pioneered there. In this photo, Rexford Tugwell (left), head of the U.S. Resettlement Administration, escorts President Franklin D. Roosevelt on a visit to the city (still under construction) in 1936. President Roosevelt visited Greenbelt on several occasions; Mrs. Roosevelt even more often. U.S. Farm Security Administration photo; courtesy of the Library of Congress, Prints and Photographs Division

The homes of Greenbelt were either townhouses or apartment houses. The federal government retained ownership until the early 1950s, when it sold the housing stock to a residents' cooperative. It is still cooperatively owned. Since the fifties there has been much private development—both commercial and residential—around old Greenbelt, but the New Deal core remains a "green town" as originally envisioned. U.S. Farm Security Administration photo; courtesy of the Library of Congress, Prints and Photographs Division

Greenbelt's commercial activities were centralized in a shopping mall. U.S. Farm Security Administration photo; courtesy of the Library of Congress, Prints and Photographs Division

An expanding, suburban population required urban services, and a police force was one of them. The Prince George's County Police Department was established in 1931 with eleven officers, and eleven Ford Tudor sedans. Pictured here, in the early thirties, are Chief Jeremiah Crowley (center) and officers Ralph Brown (left) and Arthur Hepburn (right). Courtesy of the Prince George's County Police Department

One of the early responsibilities of the police force was to enforce the Prohibition laws. Chief Jeremiah Crowley (right) supervises the destruction of some moonshine—by pouring it into the branch. Courtesy of the Prince George's County Police Department

The citizens of every suburban community—and many rural ones—formed volunteer fire companies to protect their homes from fire. Some companies, like Hyattsville's, date back to the nineteenth century. This is the Capitol Heights fire department in 1933. Today, Prince George's County is served by a mixed system of professionals and volunteers. Courtesy of Blanche L. Ennis

217

CONFIRMATION CLASS MT. CALVARY CHURCH. FORESTVILLE, MD.
MAR. 12, 1933.

*N*ew schools were opened every year in Prince George's County to serve the many children of the new suburbanites. Mount Rainier High School was one of them, opened in September 1930. Most recently a junior high school, it is now closed, for there are fewer children in the neighborhood than there used to be. The original building was a handsome one, located at the edge of town, on Queen's Chapel Road. There it still stands, but huge additions of later years make it virtually unrecognizable. These students and teachers posed before the school when it was new. Some of the boys were beginning to forsake knickers for long pants. Courtesy of the Prince George's County Board of Education

*B*ishop John McNamara of Baltimore posed with the confirmation class of Mount Calvary Roman Catholic Church, Forestville, on March 12, 1933. Courtesy of William Oertly

*A*way from Washington, beyond the suburbs, children went to school in one- and two-room frame buildings even after World War II. This photo of an unidentified school "near Marlboro, Md." was taken by a WPA photographer in 1936. Several who have seen this photo believe it is the schoolhouse at Meadows, a village along Old Marlboro Pike. The site is now part of Andrews Air Force Base. Courtesy of the National Archives

*R*acing glory returned to the Belair estate during the ownership of William Woodward, Sr. Under his direction, Belair Stables produced many fine thoroughbreds, including Triple Crown winners Gallant Fox (1930) and Omaha (1935). Woodward (right) is pictured here with trainer Sunny Jim Fitzsimmons, probably at Saratoga. Courtesy of the Belair Stables Museum

*H*ere William Woodward, Sr., leads Omaha and jockey Willie Saunders after their victory in the rain-soaked Kentucky Derby of 1935. Sired by Gallant Fox and foaled in Kentucky, Omaha was trained at Belair under the watchful eye of Sunny Jim Fitzsimmons. In the 1960s, the new city of Bowie was built upon Woodward's horse farm, but his impressive brick stables still stand, now a museum devoted to the history of racing and the Belair estate. Courtesy of the *Courier-Journal* and the *Louisville Times* archives, Louisville, Kentucky

A contestant attempts to spear a suspended ring with his lance in this jousting tournament in Accokeek in 1937. Jousting—or the ring tournament—is the official state sport of Maryland. It first became popular here in the decades before the Civil War, particularly after the publication of Sir Walter Scott's novel, *Ivanhoe*. Tournaments are still held in Prince George's County and other areas of Maryland, often with the elaborate chivalric ritual so popular in the nineteenth century. U.S. Farm Security Administration photo; courtesy of the Library of Congress, Prints and Photographs Division

The dapper little man who directed the big casino" was the way the *Evening Star* remembered Jimmy LaFontaine, one of the colorful figures in Prince George's County's recent past. During the twenties, thirties, and forties, Jimmy ran the preeminent gambling establishment in the Washington area. Located on the corner of Eastern Avenue and Bladensburg Road, it was just out of the reach of District of Columbia law enforcement officials and safely inside more tolerant Prince George's. Jimmy died in 1949. One year later, the voters elected a county government pledged to crack down on all the gambling going on in Prince George's, and the free-wheeling era came to an end. *Washington Star* photo, copyright *Washington Post*; courtesy of the District of Columbia Public Library

While most of the county's grand mansions were built in the eighteenth and nineteenth centuries, a few have been built in the twentieth. This 1929 photo shows Langley Park, completed in 1924. Designed by George Oakley Totten, Jr., it was built for Frederick and Henrietta McCormick-Goodhart and named for the Goodhart estate in England. The McCormick-Goodhart heirs sold off the handsome country estate for suburban development (Langley Park) and for a while the mansion was the headquarters of the Eudist Fathers. The house now stands in deteriorating condition, surrounded by apartment buildings, at the head of Fifteenth Avenue. *Washington Star* photo, copyright *Washington Post;* courtesy of the District of Columbia Public Library

Green Hill, near Hyattsville, appears to date from the 1920s or 1930s, but behind this facade is a stone house built in the 1860s. George Washington Riggs, founder of Riggs National Bank in Washington, built the old stone house as a country home. His grandson, Elisha Francis Riggs, transformed it into a mansion. Green Hill was built on what was once the Digges plantation, Chilham Castle Manor. The Pallotine Fathers now own the house and use it as a seminary. Courtesy of James C. Wilfong, Jr.

*E*lisha Francis Riggs is shown at a marker denoting the original gravesite of Pierre L'Enfant on the grounds of Green Hill. L'Enfant, who designed the city of Washington, lived with William Dudley Digges on the old Chilham Castle plantation during the last years of his life, and died there in 1825. His remains rested at Green Hill until 1909, when they were removed to Arlington National Cemetery. Riggs himself met a tragic end. He was assassinated by terrorists in Puerto Rico in 1936, where he was serving as chief of insular police. He was the last of the Riggs to live at Green Hill. Courtesy of the Library of Congress, Prints and Photographs Division

*F*ifteen miles from the United States Capitol, Upper Marlboro is yet to be overtaken by suburban development. The traveler reaches town, from any direction, only after passing through miles of pleasant countryside. This was Main Street in 1947, and it doesn't look much different today. First-time visitors express wonder that this small town is the seat of a county of more than 700,000 residents. Courtesy of Blanche L. Ennis

*T*he county courthouse on Main Street, Upper Marlboro, is framed by the porch of the old Marlborough House hotel in this 1949 view. The present courthouse was built in 1940; the old Victorian structure of 1881 is embedded within. The Marlborough House (long gone) was an antique shop when this photo was taken. Mr. Percy Duvall, who ran the place, was a familiar part of the Upper Marlboro scene for many years. He could usually be found in this rocking chair. *Washington Star* photo, copyright *Washington Post*; courtesy of the District of Columbia Public Library

*T*obacco buyers follow the auctioneer from one burden of tobacco to another at this loose-leaf auction in Upper Marlboro in May 1956. Prince George's tobacco has been sold at loose-leaf auctions since 1939, when the old method of selling by the hogshead began to be phased out. Growers sell the previous year's crop every spring; almost half the crop may go to Swiss and German firms, which favor the strong, slow-burning Maryland tobacco. Maryland tobacco is blended into American cigarettes only in very small proportions. Courtesy of M. E. Warren

*M*rs. Ryland Holmes, an agricultural home demonstration agent, inspects a turkey held by Mrs. Samuel Crawford, a farmer in Mitchellville. Besides their popularity at Thanksgiving time, turkeys once had an important role in the production of tobacco; they were set loose in the fields every summer to combat the worms which attacked the tobacco plants. Pesticides now do that. This picture was taken in 1956. U.S. Information Agency photo; courtesy of the National Archives

A farmer and his sons are harvesting alfalfa in Accokeek in 1949. U.S. Information Agency photo; courtesy of the National Archives

*T*he dynamic leader of the University of Maryland during the thirties, forties, and early fifties was its president, Harry Clifton Byrd. Byrd came to College Park as a student in 1905 and became president thirty years later. He had remarkable talent for extracting money from the legislature and the federal government; the University's budget grew from three to twenty million dollars during his tenure in office. A forceful and engaging personality, "Curly" Byrd transformed a small university into one of the largest in the nation. He is pictured here (on the left) escorting John M. Carmody, head of the Federal Works Agency, through some of the university's research barns in 1939. Byrd aggressively courted federal officials, and many of the buildings on the College Park campus were built with federal funds. U.S. Works Progress Administration photo; courtesy of the National Archives

*P*art of the University of Maryland campus is shown in the 1940s. The two large buildings are H. J. Patterson Hall (right) and the old Bureau of Mines (left); in the foreground is Saint Mary's Hall, a dormitory. Most striking is what's missing from the picture: Cole Field House, the Student Union, the Zoo-Psych Building, Hornbake Library, and the chemistry, physics, mathematics, and engineering buildings. There already were 10,000 students on campus; that number has tripled now. Courtesy of the Prince George's County Historical Society

226

*O*verlooking the Potomac River is Oxon Hill Manor, a forty-nine-room mansion designed by Jules Henri de Sibour. Completed in 1929, it was built for Sumner Welles, who became assistant secretary and then under secretary of state in the Franklin D. Roosevelt administration. Roosevelt was a frequent guest here. Oxon Hill Manor was built on the old Addison estate of the same name; the ruins of the old Addison house are not far away. When the federal government began searching for a vice-presidential residence in the early 1970s, Oxon Hill Manor was one of several houses considered. Now owned by the Maryland-National Capital Park and Planning Commission, it is open for tours and receptions. Historic American Buildings Survey photograph; courtesy of the Library of Congress, Prints and Photographs Division

Sumner Welles built Oxon Hill Manor. Courtesy of the Library of Congress, Prints and Photographs Division

*F*red Maloof bought Oxon Hill Manor from the Welles family in 1952 and owned it until his death in 1972. An avid art collector, he filled the house with his many acquisitions. This is the library, paneled in warm pine. It offers only a hint of the richness of the home's interior. Historic American Buildings Survey photo; courtesy of the Library of Congress, Prints and Photographs Division

Streetcars, buses, automobiles, and Christmas shoppers crowd Washington's F Street (looking west at 11th) in December 1945. Downtown Washington, with its department stores and specialty shops, was still the mecca for Prince George's County shoppers when this picture was taken. Within another ten or fifteen years' time, however, those department stores and shops would be opening branches in suburban malls, making downtown shopping a thing of the past for suburbanites. Prince George's Plaza in Hyattsville was the first large mall to open in this county. It opened in 1959. Courtesy of the District of Columbia Public Library

Suburban Prince George's County is too big—and its population too dispersed—to have one commercial center or downtown like a city does. During the 1930s and 1940s, however, Route One in Hyattsville served as the downtown for the towns of the county's old suburban corridor. This is Hyattsville in its heyday, on Route One, in 1939. Downtown Hyattsville faded in the 1950s and 1960s in the face of the competition of modern suburban malls and shopping centers, but it seems to be reviving today—just as interest in the old Victorian residential sections is on the upswing. U.S. Bureau of Public Roads photo; courtesy of the National Archives

*H*yattsville Hardware, on Baltimore Avenue, was already an institution when this photograph was taken in 1940. Established around 1910, it went out of business in 1992. U.S. Farm Security Administration photo; courtesy of the Library of Congress, Prints and Photographs Division

*L*aurel also boomed in the 1930s and 1940s. Many commuters traveled into Washington to work; the growth of nearby Fort Meade, in Anne Arundel County, also contributed. This is Washington Boulevard (now southbound Route One) in 1939. U.S. Bureau of Public Roads photo; courtesy of the National Archives

Save for the cotton mills at Laurel, there has been little large-scale manufacturing activity in Prince George's County. The ERCO plant in Riverdale was one of the exceptions. It produced Ercoupe airplanes for the Engineering Research Corporation. During World War II, it switched to the production of war materiel. After the war, the popularity of the Ercoupe planes faded, and the factory eventually closed. The building now serves as a maps and chart depot for the U.S. National Oceanic and Atmospheric Administration. Its long front facade is quite stylish for a factory; it was designed in the Art Deco style popular in the 1920s and 1930s. Courtesy of the Riversdale Society

Many residents will remember the frequent floods of the Anacostia River. The Army Corps of Engineers finally began tackling the problem in 1954 and completed a major flood control project several years later. This photo, from the 1940s, was taken in Bladensburg, at the intersection of Baltimore Avenue and Annapolis Road. In the background is Peace Cross, a World War I memorial. Courtesy of the District of Columbia Public Library

*T*hree men dominated Prince George's County politics in the 1930s and 1940s, years which saw the Democratic Party emerge as the controlling party here after six decades of power-sharing with the Republicans. Lansdale G. Sasscer (left), state senator and U.S. representative, was the acknowledged head of the county's Democratic Party. A courtly gentleman in the old Southern Maryland tradition, he was eulogized by one Washington newspaper as "the very embodiment of the seignorial system that ruled Maryland's counties for generations." T. Howard Duckett (next to Sasscer) never held elective office himself, but his influence was far-reaching. He organized the Washington Suburban Sanitary Commission and the Park and Planning Commission, served concurrently on both, and guided the development of the county's suburbs. The third member of the triumvirate was M. Hampton Magruder (right). Franklin D. Roosevelt appointed him collector of internal revenue for Maryland. The three are pictured here with Perry O. Wilkinson, a leader of the next generation, who became speaker of the Maryland House of Delegates in 1959. Sasscer, Duckett, and Magruder were members of the county's oldest families. Sasscer and Magruder were Upper Marlboro attorneys who represented the older, rural Prince George's County; Duckett was a Hyattsville lawyer and banker who shaped the new. Courtesy of the Prince George's County Historical Society

*T*his was a meeting of the Seat Pleasant Lions Club in 1947. The speaker was Robert E. Ennis of Capitol Heights. Courtesy of Blanche L. Ennis

*T*he graceful administration buildings of the Beltsville Agricultural Research Center symbolize the federal presence in Prince George's County. During the past fifty years, several major federal installations have located in the county, providing employment for thousands and promoting suburban growth. The Beltsville Agricultural Research Center is the hub of the U.S. Department of Agriculture's many research programs. Its farms, forests, orchards, and gardens occupy thousands of acres in the northern part of the county, providing much needed open space in a heavily developed region. Research began at Beltsville in 1910 , when the Department of Agriculture purchased a 475-acre farm for husbandry and dairying programs. More land was purchased and more programs were established over the years, and in 1934 they were unified administratively as the Beltsville Research Center. Courtesy of the National Archives

*P*erhaps the most famous product of the Beltsville Agricultural Research Center is the Beltsville small white turkey. It was bred with Thanksgiving in mind, with lots of meat on the breast and legs. Here, in 1942, U.S. Department of Agriculture biologist John C. Hammond carefully watches the traditional bronze turkey and the Beltsville white. Courtesy of the National Archives

General Curtis LeMay examines a globe at the headquarters of the Strategic Air Command, Andrews Air Force Base, in 1948. In 1942, the U.S. Army built a military airfield to serve wartime Washington in the rural community of Camp Springs, five miles southeast of the District line in Prince George's County. The Camp Springs Army Airfield eventually became Andrews Air Force Base, named for General Frank M. Andrews, the World War II commander of Army Air Force operations in Europe who was killed in an aircraft accident in 1943. Since the war, Andrews has served as headquarters of the Continental Air Command, Strategic Air Command, Military Air Transport Service, and Air Force Systems Command. Today the base occupies more than 4,000 acres of land and is home to a number of military units, including the Eighty-ninth Military Airlift Wing, which provides transportation for the president and other high-ranking officials. Andrews was a major force encouraging suburbanization in that part of Prince George's County south of the District line, an area not visited by the railroads and streetcars of an earlier era. Camp Springs — no longer the rural community of old — derives its name not from its military association, but from the Methodist camp meetings held there in the nineteenth century. The area has also been known historically as Allentown. Courtesy of United Press International, New York, New York

This was part of the crowd at an open house at Andrews Air Force Base in 1946. The open houses at Andrews have drawn the largest crowds ever to assemble in this county; 300,000 attended the 1990 show. As the ceremonial air gateway to the nation's capital, Andrews has also welcomed many foreign dignitaries — Pope John Paul II among them — as well as returning prisoners of war from Vietnam (1973) and the Americans held hostage in Iran (1981). Courtesy of the District of Columbia Public Library

233

A car pool prepares to depart for Washington from Greenbelt during the 1940s. Courtesy of the Library of Congress, Prints and Photographs Division

*T*his was a modern supermarket in Bladensburg in 1950. The age of the general store was over, at least in the populous suburbs. This store was the Acme Supermarket on Annapolis Road. U.S. Information Agency photo; courtesy of the National Archives

Turkey Tayac leads a Full Harvest Moon ceremony in 1951. Tayac was born a member of the Proctor family in Charles County. He led the movement among the Piscataway people of Southern Maryland to reestablish a tribal identity and adopt Indian customs. He died in 1978 at the age of eighty-three and was buried, with special permission of Congress, in the ancient Indian burial grounds in Piscataway National Park. *U.S. Information Agency photo; courtesy of the National Archives*

Women have been active in fire departments and rescue squads for many years. Lita Nixon, Mona Tillman, and Joan Tillman, of Laurel, prepare this ambulance for service in 1954. *Washington Star* photo, copyright *Washington Post;* courtesy of the District of Columbia Public Library

This is a scene that seems to symbolize the 1950s: cheerleaders and a football star. Here Jack Severn, a letterman on Bladensburg High School's football team, is introduced by the Bladensburg cheerleaders at the Football Hop, September 1957. From left to right, the cheerleaders are Elaine Montague, Joan Culver, Jean Fritter, Carol Lettman, Dale Devey, Gloria Palazzo, co-captain Esther Annandale, and captain Carol Thrift. *Prince George's Post* photo; courtesy of the Prince George's County Historical Society

University of Maryland football coach Tommy Mont greets Prince Philip as Queen Elizabeth, Governor Theodore McKeldin, and a full house at Byrd Stadium look on, prior to the Maryland-North Carolina football game in October 1957. The game is remembered as "The Queen's Game," and Queen Elizabeth later stated that it was the highlight of her 1957 American tour. Although the glory days of Maryland football were past (years which saw Maryland win the national championship in 1951), the Terrapins defeated the favored Tarheels 21-7. Courtesy of the Prince George's County Historical Society

Development of the Suitland area was spurred by the building of the Suitland Federal Center in the early 1940s. Suitland was still a semi-rural community then, but within a few years apartment complexes, housing developments, and shopping centers would follow. The Census Bureau, with its headquarters at Suitland, has been the principal occupant of the center, but other agencies (notably the old Naval Hydrographic Office) have also had offices there over the years. This photograph dates from the late 1950s. Silver Hill Road runs vertically through the center of the picture; Suitland Road runs horizontally. The view is toward the northeast. Courtesy of the Columbia Historical Society

Officers of the Kiwanis Club of Prince George's County gather in New Carrollton in 1958 for the ground breaking of the Kiwanis Club's Home of the Year—a house to be sold to benefit the club's charitable projects. At the controls that day was Jesse Baggett, county commissioner and president of the Kiwanis. Others in the picture (from left to right) are Leonard H. Burch; Delegate Hervey G. Machen; George Langhenry; State Senator H. Winship Wheatley, Jr.; T. Hammond Welsh, Jr.; S. Walter Bogley; York D. Hollingsworth; Herbert W. Wells; Harry D. Eisenhauer; and Richard G. Milbourne. New Carrollton was the largest single development project begun in this county before 1960. Its builder was Albert Turner, a native of Hyattsville. *Prince George's Post* photo; courtesy of the Prince George's County Historical Society

The winners of a Palmer Park beauty contest prepare for a parade in the early 1960s. Courtesy of the Prince George's County Historical Society

During the suburban era, houses replaced tobacco as the cash crop in much of Prince George's County. This is William J. Levitt's harvest of 1962 — part of his huge development, Belair at Bowie, built on the historic Belair estate. Belair at Bowie was built far beyond the existing suburbs; its center, on Annapolis Road, is less than two miles from the Patuxent River. The first families began moving into Levitt homes at Belair in 1961; the first was the family of Edward T. Conroy, later a state senator. A semi-rural countryside still intervenes between Belair and the close-in suburbs, although the city of Bowie has grown considerably beyond the original development at Belair. It is now the county's largest municipality, home of more than 30,000 residents. *Washington Star* photo, copyright *Washington Post*, courtesy of the District of Columbia Public Library

*T*he cloverleaf at the intersection of Indian Head Highway (in Oxon Hill) and the unfinished Beltway is shown in 1962. The Potomac River is in the background. The Beltway (which circles Washington, D.C.) is the major highway link between the suburbs of northern and southern Prince George's County. Before the Beltway was opened in 1964, a trip between the two sections involved a drive through Washington or an even longer, winding journey across various country roads. U.S. Bureau of Public Roads photo; courtesy of the National Archives

The 1960s are remembered as years of social change, particularly in the area of race relations. These members of Prince George's County's Congress of Racial Equality (CORE) marched in front of the model homes of William J. Levitt's Belair development after sales agents there refused to sell a home to a black couple. The segregated restaurants on Route One were also frequent targets of protests and sit-ins. National and state civil rights laws eventually brought the discriminatory practices to an end. *Washington Star* photo; copyright *Washington Post;* courtesy of the District of Columbia Public Library

The National Guard was sent to the University of Maryland campus in May 1970 to keep Route One open after hundreds of students protesting the Vietnam War blocked the roadway for several hours. Guardsmen returned the following spring, too, when protesters seized the road again. These Guardsmen took positions along Route One below the chapel on the evening of May 4, 1970. They had dispersed several crowds gathering on the chapel lawn with tear gas earlier that day. *Washington Star* photo, copyright *Washington Post;* courtesy of the District of Columbia Public Library

School busing for racial integration became part of the county's educational program in 1973 by order of Judge Frank A. Kaufman, a federal judge in Baltimore. Although Prince George's County abolished its dual school system in 1965, many schools, particularly the neighborhood elementary schools, remained completely or predominantly of one race because of residential patterns. Judge Kaufman ordered a massive school busing program, removing thousands of students from their neighborhood schools and sending them to schools miles away. Thirty-three thousand students were transferred on January 29, 1973, in the middle of the school year. These students are arriving at Longfields Elementary School, Forestville, in the first week of busing. *Washington Star* photo, copyright *Washington Post;* courtesy of the District of Columbia Public Library

Governor George C. Wallace of Alabama brought his campaign for the Democratic nomination for the presidency to Prince George's County in May 1972, speaking at several locations, including Capital Plaza and the Laurel Shopping Center. This photograph was taken at his rally in Laurel on May 15. Within minutes he was sprawled on the parking lot blacktop, shot by Arthur Bremer of Milwaukee, Wisconsin. Though he survived the shooting. Wallace would never walk again. He won both the Maryland and Michigan primaries the next day. *Washington Star* photo, copyright *Washington Post;* courtesy of the District of Columbia Public Library

241

*L*ocated along the Beltway in Largo, the Capital Centre has been the scene of many notable events, including concerts by Frank Sinatra and Elvis Presley, prizefights by Muhammed Ali and Sugar Ray Leonard, and the Inaugural galas for Presidents Reagan and Clinton. Abe Pollin built the Capital Centre in 1973 to be the home of his basketball and hockey franchises, the Washington Bullets and the Washington Capitals. The teams played here until 1997, when they moved to a new arena in downtown Washington. Sugar Ray Leonard's 1980 title defense was of particular local interest, as the welterweight champion grew up only a few miles away in Palmer Park. Courtesy of Capital Centre

*T*his is the County Administration Building in Upper Marlboro, as seen from the walkway around Schoolhouse Pond. The building was dedicated in 1977. Photo by the author

*R*apid rail transit came to Prince George's County with the opening of Metrorail's Orange line to New Carrollton in 1978. The Blue line to Addison Road (Seat Pleasant) followed two years later; the Green Line to Greenbelt opened in 1993. A line into southern Prince George's County will open early in the new century. Thousands of commuters ride the Metro to work in Washington every day, just as Prince Georgeans of an earlier generation rode the streetcars. This Orange line train is heading into Washington, having just left the Landover station. The old Pennsylvania Railroad tracks (which now carry Amtrak trains) are at the left. Photo by the author

*R*ural land gives way to development in southern Prince George's County. This is a scene in Marlton, a planned community along Route 301 southwest of Upper Marlboro. The photo was taken in 1981. *Washington Star* photo, copyright *Washington Post;* courtesy of the District of Columbia Public Library

*T*his is a reminder of our past—a barn full of tobacco near Upper Marlboro. After more than three hundred years of settlement, tobacco is still grown and cured in Prince George's County, despite the many changes three centuries have witnessed. Courtesy of M. E. Warren

*V*isitors have passed through this door at Montpelier for more than 200 years. The path through the box leads to the Patuxent River. Historic American Buildings Survey photo; courtesy of the Library of Congress, Prints and Photographs Division

Chapter 10

PRINCE GEORGE'S COUNTY IN THE EIGHTIES AND NINETIES

On St. George's Day, April 23, 1996, Prince Georgeans celebrated the 300th anniversary of the founding of their county. Early in the morning, a commemorative program led by the governor and county executive was held at historic Mount Calvert, on the Patuxent River, site of the first court meeting three centuries before. The entire judiciary of Prince George's County assembled on the lawn and convened in special session in tribute to the first court that brought Prince George's County into being there in 1696. At noon, a military march and review wound through the streets of Upper Marlboro, down Main Street in front of the courthouse, just as innumerable parades had done in years past. In the evening, a gala dinner-dance was held at Cole Field House on the campus of the University of Maryland in College Park. From the rural countryside of south county to the urban environs of the Washington suburbs, Prince George's County's Tricentennial was celebrated in a style befitting a county so very much aware of its historic past.

"Semper Eadem" is the motto of Prince George's County. In Latin, it means "Ever the Same." Nothing could be further from the truth. Prince George's County is ever-changing. In the eighteenth century, tobacco, planters, and slaves transformed a rough, egalitarian frontier into an ordered and wealthy plantation economy. In the nineteenth, civil war and emancipation freed a people but plunged the county into a state of economic decline. But then in the twentieth century, the expanding federal government brought in thousands of new residents, spurring the suburban growth that remade Prince George's County into a dynamic metropolitan community of three quarter of a million souls. So if there is one constant in Prince George's County's history, it is change. "Ever the Same" means "Ever Changing."

During the 1980s and 1990s, no element of change was so pronounced or so visible as the increase and empowerment of Prince George's County's black population. Before the Civil War, blacks constituted more than half of Prince George's population. Twentieth-century suburbanization, which until the 1970s was mainly a white phenomenon, reduced the black percentage to less than five percent. But open housing and civil rights laws, coupled with traditionally less expensive housing than other suburban jurisdictions, attracted new, largely middle-class black residents throughout the 1970s, 80s, and

90s. As the new century and new millennium dawn, Prince George's County's population is estimated to be approximately 56 percent black and 39 percent white. Small but vibrant communities of immigrants from Vietnam and other Asian nations, as well as Spanish-speaking newcomers from Latin America (concentrated particularly in Langley Park), add even more diversity to the mosaic of Prince George's County.

The transformation from a predominantly white, middle-and-working-class county into a more diverse community with a black majority occurred peacefully, though not without some tension. Many white families left the county to avoid the school busing imposed by a federal court in 1972, and racial bickering occasionally erupted in the local press. Nevertheless, Prince George's County in the eighties and nineties earned a national reputation as model of toleration and diversity. The 1990 *Almanac of American Politics* declared Prince George's County to be "one of the nation's most important counties—and a place that gives a hopeful glimpse of a possible future." One of the chief reasons for that praise was the relatively smooth integration of blacks into the higher levels of the county's economic and political structure. The new black majority is, in the main, middle class and affluent. During the 1980s and 90s, blacks assumed their rightful places in the community associations, business clubs, law firms, police force, County Council, judiciary, and the legislature—virtually all segments of public, social, and civic life. The election of Wayne K. Curry as county executive in 1994, the first African American to hold that office, symbolized the new era.

Proceeding apace with the social change in the eighties and nineties was the growth of the county's economy. Once characterized as a bedroom community for Washington, D.C., Prince George's County in the eighties and nineties boasted an economy that was growing and diversifying. Although the 1990s were not as heady years as the 1980s, economic progress was the hallmark of both decades.

"It's impossible to deny that the county is in the midst of an economic awakening," wrote the *Washingtonian* magazine in May 1986, declaring Prince George's County to be the "up-and-coming neighbor" of the metropolitan area. Proximity to both Washington and Baltimore, attractive prices for land, plentiful building sites along its interstate highways, and an aggressive economic development program all contributed to an economic boom in the 1980s. The new buildings that arose across the county were not the strip shopping centers of old, but towering office complexes and landscaped business campuses housing national and international firms. The county's Economic Development Corporation issued a guide to "Executive Housing" for the new corporate officers, while regional magazines like the *Washingtonian* and *Regardie's* featured upbeat, almost boosterish, reports on the economic progress in Prince George's County.

Such progress did not come without problems, however. Prince George's County experienced growing pains. Though the county's road system is conceded to be the least-congested in the metropolitan area, that was little solace to residents experiencing urban-style traffic conditions for the first time. The intrusion of office parks and new residential communities into the old rural countryside of east and south county vexed quite a few; "No Growth" and "Slow Growth" became the rallying cries for a powerful corps of citizen activists. Balancing economic growth with environmental and esthetic considerations became a tightwire act for county officials; compromise became the byword.

Just as dramatic as the progress in the sphere of economic development was the progress in the field of education. The busing controversies of the 1970s bruised the image of the Prince George's County public schools; innovative educational programs of the 1980s did much to rehabilitate that image. Magnet schools became a cornerstone of the academic program, offering specialized instruction at almost fifty school sites. These special programs ranged from Montessori, foreign language immersion, and classical training in the lower grades, to high schools for the arts, humanities, and sciences for older students. And in 1998, the federal court, with the endorsement of the county NAACP, mercifully agreed that it was time to end school busing. After twenty-five years, the rationale for school busing had evaporated. With the changing demographics of the county, the school busing program was mainly transporting black children from one black-majority school to another. The return to the neighborhood school concept puts to rest one of the more potent reminders of a divisive past.

If any one problem plagued the county most in the eighties and nineties, it was the problem of drug-induced crime. Drugs, particularly crack cocaine, flooded into Prince George's County, contributing to an epidemic of crime in the lower-income neighborhoods. While the crime rate remained significantly lower than the District of Columbia's, the figures were still shocking by Prince George's County standards. The homicide count soared to 140 in 1995, more than double the number of a decade before. Most of the deaths were drug-related, most took place inside the Beltway, and most of the victims were young black males. In July of 1990, the Rand Corporation's Drug Policy Research Center estimated that there were 24,000 dealers in the city of Washington peddling 350 million dollars worth of drugs annually. The resignation of the chairman of the Prince George's County Council, upon indictment on drug charges that same summer, highlighted the problem. But the crack cocaine epidemic seemed to subside, and in the late 1990s, the crime rate began to drop.

Despite its share of urban and suburban problems, Prince George's County enters its fourth century prosperous and diverse. But while survey after survey ranks Prince George's as one of the nation's most affluent counties, regionally that is often forgotten. The shadows cast by Montgomery and Fairfax counties—two jurisdictions that compete annually for the title of "Nation's Richest"—are long ones. Prince George's County gained a reputation as a rough-and-tumble working class suburb of Washington during its period of massive growth at mid-century. That reputation lingers. "It's simply the kind of place where most people prefer beer to champagne," wrote the *Washington Post* in January 1981, in an article that ruffled quite a few local feathers. But most who live and work in Prince George's County are less concerned with image than reality. They know Prince George's County to be a heterogeneous community with diverse neighborhoods—rich, poor, but mostly middle class; rural, urban, but mostly suburban. The diversity of the 1980s and 90s mirrors the diversity of three centuries before, when English, Scots, Africans, Irish, and Indians, all speaking dialects scarcely intelligible to each other, all with different customs, histories, and manners of worship, were thrown together on the Maryland frontier and, however imperfectly, began the story of Prince George's County. The 1986 *Washingtonian* magazine article described Prince George's County as "more like the real America" than any other jurisdiction in the Washington area. Prince Georgeans in the new century will know it as it was described by the *Almanac of American Politics* in 1990: a "productive, tolerant, attractive community."

Mount Airy, the colonial home of the Calvert family (page 62 to 64), stands as a symbol of Prince George's County's architectural heritage. Owned by the State of Maryland, it was restored by Frank and Patricia Kulla and opened as a country inn and restaurant in 1985. Photograph by Phil Masturzo, courtesy of the *Prince George's Journal*

Scientific research is a vital part of Prince George's County's new economy. Goddard Space Flight Center, a NASA facility in Greenbelt, plays an important role in the nation's space program as a communications, research, and weather center. Goddard was opened in 1959 and named in honor of Robert Goddard, father of American rocketry. Courtesy of National Aeronautics and Space Administration

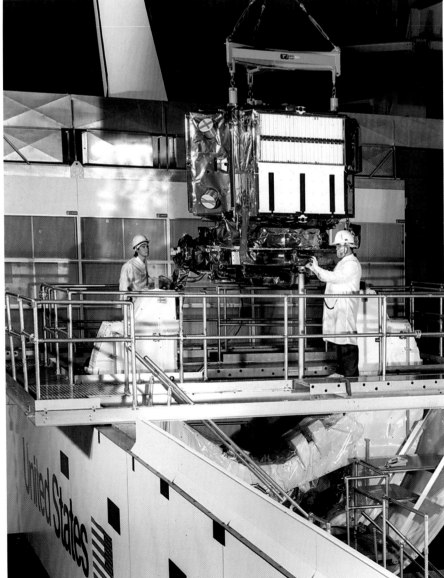

Metro's Green Line into northern Prince George's County opened in 1993. This was part of the tunnel under West Hyattsville, under construction in 1988. Photograph by Ron Ceasar, courtesy of the *Prince George's Journal*

The widening of John Hanson Highway was one of the county's many large road improvement projects of the 1980s and 1990s. A construction worker stands high above the Beltway on one of the ramps that became part of the Capital Beltway interchange. Photograph by Katherine Frey, courtesy of the *Prince George's Journal*

One of the county government's greatest challenges is to insure that roadbuilding keeps pace with residential and commercial development. This was the scene on a Friday afternoon in 1988 on southbound Route 5, near Brandywine in southern Prince George's County. Many of these commuters were heading home to Charles County. Photograph by Ron Ceasar, courtesy of the *Prince George's Journal*

Darnall's Chance, an early eighteenth century home in Upper Marlboro, was reborn in 1988 when it was restored to its gambrel-roofed colonial appearance. The house was probably built between the years 1700 and 1705 by Col. Henry Darnall, and it is likely that it was the birthplace of Archbishop John Carroll, whose family owned it in 1735, the year of his birth. In 1858, the house was remodeled into the Italianate style (page 113) and by 1974, when it was acquired by the county, its earlier history had been forgotten. Only after more than a decade of architectural, archeological, and historical study was its past uncovered. Darnall's Chance is the oldest building in Upper Marlboro. It is owned by the Maryland-National Capital Park and Planning Commission. Courtesy of History Division, M-NCPPC

Archeological investigations at Darnall's Chance uncovered an eighteenth-century burial vault not far from the house. Once partially above ground, the vault was filled in when the roof collapsed, probably sometime in the early nineteenth century. Archeologists found the skeletal remains of seven individuals within the vault, both children and adults. Their identities are uncertain. Courtesy of History Division, Maryland-National Capital Park and Planning Commission

The opening to the burial vault at Darnall's Chance. Photograph by Ron Ceasar, courtesy of the *Prince George's Journal*

The bachelors' footrace was a traditional part of many colonial wedding festivities. These men in colonial garb were part of a wedding held at the National Colonial Farm in Accokeek in 1989. Photograph by Katherine Frey, courtesy of the *Prince George's Journal*

Members of the Prince George's County chapter of the NAACP march toward the Capitol during the Washington civil rights rally of 1989. The local chapter of the National Association for the Advancement of Colored People was founded in the 1930s. Photograph by Katherine Frey, courtesy of the *Prince George's Journal*

These students from Magnolia Elementary School in Lanham participate in a "Say No To Drugs" rally at the Capital Centre, 1988. Photograph by Sharon Kuck, courtesy of the *Prince George's Journal*

Superintendent of schools John Murphy, left, and Jesse Jackson visit Columbia Park Elementary School in Landover on the first day of school, 1989. Since the 1960s, the Prince George's County school system has been one of the largest in the nation. Photograph by Lars Gelfan, courtesy of the *Prince George's Journal*

President Bush inspects a striped bass at PEPCO's Aquaculture Center at the company's Chalk Point power station on the Patuxent River. The president visited the plant in March 1990 during his campaign for the Clean Air Act. Chalk Point — a coal-fired plant — is one of the Potomac Electric Power Company's major generating stations. The company takes advantage of its river site to raise striped bass and yellow perch. As of 1990, it had released more than a million fish into Patuxent and Chesapeake waters. Photograph by Phil Masturzo, courtesy of the *Prince George's Journal*

The whooping crane has been rescued from the brink of extinction by the captive breeding program at the Patuxent Wildlife Research Center. Located on 4700 acres on the Patuxent River between Laurel and Bowie, the center was established by the U.S. Fish and Wildlife Service in 1936. Research into the effects of agricultural, industrial, and chemical wastes on wildlife is also an important part of the research program at Patuxent. Photograph by Katherine Frey, courtesy of the *Prince George's Journal*

Both the State of Maryland and Prince George's County have acquired large tracts of land along the Patuxent River to protect the Chesapeake Bay watershed. Much of that land has been developed into parks. This bridge crosses the marshes of Mattaponi Creek, near Croom. It is part of a driving tour that seeks to inform the public of the importance of the Patuxent wetlands to the ecology of the Chesapeake Bay. Photograph by Sharon Kuck, courtesy of the *Prince George's Journal*

*C*itizens in urban areas across the country have united to fight crime by forming citizen patrols. This group in Riverdale is one of many in Prince George's County. Courtesy of the *Prince George's Journal*

*S*uspects are apprehended in a drug raid in Landover, 1988. Photograph by Lon Slepicka, courtesy of the *Prince George's Journal*

*T*he Prince George's County Fair, first held in 1842, is one of the oldest fairs in the nation. Though Prince George's is not the agricultural county of old, the traditional late-summer event still draws thousands to Upper Marlboro every year to enjoy agricultural exhibits, entertainment, and the carnival midway. Photograph by Ron Ceasar, courtesy of the *Prince George's Journal*

*T*he ring tournament attracts participants of all ages. This tournament took place at the county's Equestrian Center in Upper Marlboro. Developed by the county government at the old Marlboro Race Track site, the center hosts a wide variety of equestrian events, including jousting tournaments, polo matches, and horse shows. It also serves as a training and stabling facility. The county acquired the site in 1980 and opened the center in 1982. Courtesy of the *Prince George's Journal*

The green leaves of tobacco in August are almost ready for harvest. These visitors have gathered for an exhibition on tobacco growing at the University of Maryland's experimental farm in Largo. Photograph by Sharon Kuck, courtesy of the *Prince George's Journal*

*A*waiting the auctioneer in one of the tobacco warehouses in Upper Marlboro. Tobacco farming declined sharply in Prince George's County during the 1980s. The 1987 federal census of agriculture revealed that for the first time, tobacco had lost its position as the county's chief cash crop. The market value of fruits and vegetables now exceeds that of tobacco. The state tobacco warehouse at Cheltenham, in southern Prince George's County, has been converted to a retail and wholesale farmers produce market. Courtesy of the *Prince George's Journal*

*R*epresentative of the diversity in Prince George's County is this Hindu temple in Lanham. Construction of the Sri Siva Vishnu Temple was begun in 1988. It incorporates several styles of temple architecture and is one of the largest Hindu temples in the Western hemisphere. The Buddhist and Muslim religions are two other ancient faiths also newly represented in Prince George's County. Photograph by Susan Pearl

*T*he Justice Center in downtown Hyattsville is the center of judicial and law enforcement activities in northern Prince George's County. Built adjacent to the old County Service Building, it was dedicated in August 1990. Courtesy of Grimm & Parker, Architects

*G*overnor Parris N. Glendening, County Executive Wayne K. Curry, and Tricentennial Celebration Committee Chairman Timothy F. Maloney pause with the colonial court crier on the lawn at Mount Calvert, site of the first county courthouse, on St. George's Day, April 23, 1996, the three hundredth anniversary of the establishment of Prince George's County. A former county executive, Glendening was elected governor in 1994, the first Prince Georgean chosen for that office since Oden Bowie in 1867. Photograph by Steve Abramowitz, courtesy of the Maryland-National Capital Park and Planning Commission

*T*he Sheriff's color guard bearing the national, state, and county colors marches down Main Street in Upper Marlboro in the Tricentennial March and Military Review, on April 23, 1996. Photograph by Steve Abramowitz; courtesy of the Maryland-National Capital Park and Planning Commission

*C*ounty Executive Wayne K. Curry speaks to an audience assembled for the Tricentennial March and Military Review. A lifelong resident of Prince George's County, Curry was elected in 1994 as the fifth county executive under charter government. He is the first African American to hold that post. Photograph by Steve Abramowitz; courtesy of the Maryland-National Capital Park and Planning Commission

During the War of 1812, Commodore Joshua Barney fought the British Navy in the Chesapeake with small craft like this one. He scuttled his flotilla in the Patuxent River to prevent its capture when the British began their march across Prince George's County (pages 94–97). During the Tricentennial year, the Maryland-National Capital Park and Planning Commission built this replica of Commodore Barney's barge. Launched in Bladensburg, it is seen here on the Patuxent, before Mount Calvert, in September 1996. Photograph by Steve Abramowitz; courtesy of the Maryland-National Capital Park and Planning Commission

Commodore Barney's barge was built with the assistance of high school and middle school students from Prince George's County. Photograph by Steve Abramowitz; courtesy of the Maryland-National Capital Park and Planning Commission

*T*his quilt, depicting scenes from Prince George's County, was made by county employees in honor of the Tricentennial. It hangs in the County Administration Building. Photograph by Steve Abramowitz; courtesy of the Maryland-National Capital Park and Planning Commission

*T*hree bronze horses in mid-gallop welcome visitors to the county courthouse in Upper Marlboro. Entitled "Tricentennial," the sculpture by Raymond Kaskey symbolizes the three centuries of Prince George's history. The horses stand in front of the new addition to the courthouse. Completed in 1991, the new building faces south, toward the Western Branch, and is larger than the old courthouse on Main Street. Copyright Kaskey Studio, Inc., and Prince George's County, Maryland, 1996. All rights reserved.

*S*culptor Raymond Kaskey, at right, supervises the mounting of the three horses before the new south front of the county courthouse. Copyright Kaskey Studio, Inc., and Prince George's County, Maryland, 1996.

*C*olonial Governor Francis Nicholson (as portrayed by Cecil Thompson) attended many of the events during the Tricentennial year. Photo by Steve Abramowitz; courtesy of Maryland-National Capital Park and Planning Commission

*T*he Washington Redskins moved to Prince George's County with the opening of Jack Kent Cooke Stadium in Landover in September 1997. Named for the longtime owner of the football team, the stadium sits high on a hill near what was once the Brightseat crossroads. Courtesy of the Washington Redskins

A winter's scene along Westphalia Road, not far from Upper Marlboro. This is the site of the old Dunblane plantation. Generations past rest in the snow-covered burial ground as children of the present enjoy a day off from school. Photograph by Phil Masturzo, courtesy of the *Prince George's Journal*

THE PRINCE GEORGE'S COUNTY HISTORICAL SOCIETY

Framed by boxwood, holly, and pecan trees, Marietta is situated on a ridge overlooking its current twenty-five acres of woods and agricultural fields.

History is happening at Marietta.

Since 1985 the Prince George's County Historical Society has been headquartered at Marietta, the early nineteenth century farm on Bell Station Road in Glenn Dale, once owned by native Prince Georgean Gabriel Duvall, associate justice of the U.S. Supreme Court.

The tranquil setting—Federal plantation house, law office, and root cellar—shaded by majestic pecan, holly, osage orange, and black walnut trees, provides a picture of another age in the county. Each Sunday afternoon—and on special occasions—visitors may see the period furnishings

and gain an appreciation of domestic life in the early 1800s while Judge Duvall was in residence.

However, Marietta is not the run-of-the-mill historic house museum. It houses a library of several thousand volumes on county and Maryland history and such allied areas as architecture, art, and antiques. Local newspapers, photographs, maps, personal papers, and other memorabilia all add depth to the collection which is utilized by school children, genealogists, public officials, authors, and many other private citizens.

An ongoing oral history program is recording the memories of county

events and life in the twentieth century as witnessed by those who were the actors on that stage—the county's senior citizens.

Lectures at regular public meetings provide insight on the history of the county's local communities and people. A games day featuring those entertainments of yesteryears, a Mad Hatter's tea party, and a history project competition in the school system are all designed as learning experiences to help young children appreciate their local heritage.

An active publications program has produced a newsletter containing news and articles of historical interest

Tours of the home and law office of Gabriel Duvall demonstrate his dual role as planter and jurist in the early nineteenth century. The leader of this tour was the Society's longtime president, Frederick S. DeMarr

In observance of the bicentennial of the U.S. Constitution in September 1987, the remains of Judge Duvall were moved from an unmarked grave to the west lawn of Marietta by the Society of Mareen Duvall Descendants.
Photos courtesy of Warren W. Rhoads.

for the past eighteen years. Van Horn's *Out of the Past,* the *Hopkins Atlas,* the *Martenet Atlas,* and *Prince George's County: A Pictorial History* have been major contributions to the literature of local history. And, to broaden people's horizons, semi-annual tours are conducted to points of historical interest in other counties of Maryland.

In September 1990, the Association for State and Local History presented their prestigious Certificate of Commendation to the Prince George's County Historical Society for outstanding effort in the field of interpretation of local history.

The Prince George's County

Historical Society itself is steeped in history. The Society had its birth when T. Howard Duckett, a county banker and political leader, held a meeting of twelve interested citizens at the Calvert Mansion in Riverdale on September 15, 1952.

Since then, the Society has grown in numbers and in programs. And it will continue to expand to meet the needs of the future. Whether you live in Aquasco or Laurel, Upper Marlboro or Muirkirk, Clinton, University Park, or Oxon Hill, the Society invites you to share an active interest in the county's heritage. Become a member or a volunteer, attend one of the lectures, visit

Marietta, use the resources of the library. The welcome mat is out and the Society encourages volunteer efforts to keep up the momentum. Even if unfamiliar with local history, as a volunteer you learn while helping others to learn.

The Tricentennial of the founding of Prince George's County was celebrated in grand style in 1996. The Board of Directors and the Society's members join to suggest that you help us make things happen in our fourth century.

BIBLIOGRAPHY

Boucher, Jack E. *Landmarks of Prince George's County.* Baltimore: Johns Hopkins University Press, 1993.

Bowie, Effie Gwynn. *Across the Years in Prince George's County.* 1947. Reprint. Baltimore: Genealogical Publishing Company, 1975.

Brugger, Robert J. *Maryland: A Middle Temperament, 1634–1980.* Baltimore: Johns Hopkins University Press, 1988.

Clark, Charles Branch. *Politics in Maryland During the Civil War.* Chestertown, Md.: 1952.

Ferguson, Alice, and Henry G. Ferguson. *The Piscataway Indians of Southern Maryland.* Accokeek: Alice Ferguson Foundation, 1960.

Floyd, Bianca P. *Records and Recollections: Early Black History in Prince George's County, Maryland.* Riverdale: Maryland-National Capital Park and Planning Commission, 1989.

Gale, Dennis E. *Washington, D.C.: Inner-City Revitalization and Minority Suburbanization.* Philadelphia: Temple University Press, 1987.

Green, Constance McLaughlin. *Washington: A History of the Capital, 1800–1958.* 1962. Reprint. Princeton: Princeton University Press, 1976.

Hienton, Louise Joyner. *Prince George's Heritage.* Baltimore: Maryland Historical Society, 1972.

Historic Sites and Districts Plan, Prince George's County, Maryland. Upper Marlboro: Maryland-National Capital Park and Planning Commission, 1992.

Hopkins, G. M. *Atlas of Prince George's County, 1878.* Edited by Frank F. White, Jr. Reprint. Riverdale: Prince George's County Historical Society, 1975.

Howell, Joseph T. *Hard Living on Clay Street: Portraits of Blue Collar Families.* Garden City, N.Y.: Anchor Press/Doubleday, 1973.

King, LeRoy O., Jr. *100 Years of Capital Traction: The Story of Streetcars in the Nation's Capital.* College Park: Taylor Publishing Company, 1972.

Kulikoff, Allan. *Tobacco and Slaves: The Development of Southern Cultures in the Chesapeake, 1680–1800.* Chapel Hill: University of North Carolina Press, 1986.

Lord, Walter. *The Dawn's Early Light.* New York: W. W. Norton and Company, 1972.

Main, Gloria L. *Tobacco Colony: Life in Early Maryland, 1650–1720.* Princeton: Princeton University Press, 1982.

Martenet, Simon J. *Atlas of Prince George's County, Maryland, 1861.* Edited by Joyce W. McDonald. Reprint, Riverdale: Prince George's County Historical Society, 1995.

Newman, Harry Wright. *Mareen Duvall of Middle Plantation . . . and his Descendants.* Washington, D.C.: 1952.

Prince George's County Community Renewal Program. *The Neighborhoods of Prince George's County.* Upper Marlboro, Md.: 1974.

Sargent, Jean A., editor. *Stones and Bones: Cemetery Records of Prince George's County, Maryland.* Bowie: Prince George's County Genealogical Society, 1984.

Thornton, Alvin, and Karen Williams Gooden. *Like a Phoenix I'll Rise: An Illustrated History of African Americans in Prince George's County, Maryland, 1696–1996.* Virginia Beach, Va.: The Donning Company, 1997.

Tilp, Frederick. *This Was Potomac River.* Alexandria, Va.: 1978.

Van Horn, R. Lee. *Out of the Past: Prince Georgeans and Their Land.* Riverdale: Prince George's County Historical Society, 1976.

Yewell, Therese C. *Women of Achievement in Prince George's County History.* Upper Marlboro: Maryland-National Capital Park and Planning Commission, 1994.

FICTIONAL WORKS
SET IN PRINCE GEORGE'S COUNTY

Briscoe, Connie. *Sisters & Lovers.* New York: HarperCollins, 1994. A novel of three black women and suburban life.

Cain, James M. *Cloud Nine.* New York: Mysterious Press, 1984. Intrigue in Riverdale and Hyattsville. The author of *Mildred Pierce* and *The Postman Always Rings Twice* was a Maryland native. He retired to University Park after a career as a Hollywood screenwriter and novelist.

Cain, James M. *Galatea.* New York: Knopf, 1953. 242 p. "Hard-boiled" novel set in Prince George's County.

Cain, James M. "Pay-off Girl." *Esquire*, August 1952. Short story about gambling and romance in Prince George's County.

Cook, Ebenezer. *The Sot-weed Factor: or, A Voyage to Maryland.* 1708. 21 p. Reprint. A satire, in verse, which begins with the factor's arrival in Piscataway.

DeBlasis, Celeste. *Wild Swan.* New York: Bantam Books, 1984. Historical novel of romance and thoroughbred racing in the nineteenth century. The plantation Wild Swan is identified as being in Prince George's County; it is based upon Belair.

Mewshaw, Michael. *Man in Motion.* New York: Random House, 1970. 247 p. A modern novel set in Prince George's County by a novelist who grew up here.

INDEX

Palo Alto Hotel, 159
Parthenon, 179
Patterson, Elizabeth, 62
Patuxent River, 138, 140, 258, 267
Patuxent River plantations, 43, 46, 72, 99, 106, 184, 245
Patuxent Wildlife Research Center, 258
Peace Cross, 43, 54, 230
Peale, Charles Willson, 79
Penn's Mill, 57
Pennsylvania Railroad, 143, 243
Perrie family, 163
Phelps, Edward, 154
Piscataway, 39, 40, 166, 171, 178
Piscataway Creek, 19, 41
Piscataway House, 57
Piscataway Indians, 19, 22, 28, 166, 235
Planters' Advocate, 116, 120, 124
Planters' Guard, 123
Plummer family, 136
Police, 216, 217, 259
Pope's Creek Line, 140, 143
Poplar Hill, 65
Potomac (steamboat), 157
Potomac River plantations, 35, 48
Pratt, Thomas, 86, 110
Presbyterians, 41, 61, 88, 110
Prince George's Bank, 209
Prince Georgian, 124, 142
Proctor family, 235
Prohibition, 159, 196, 197, 217

Q
Queen Anne, Md., 39, 40, 102
Queen family, 88

R
Reagan, Ronald, 242
Red Cross, 180
Religious history, 18, 19, 29, 30, 41, 86, 88, 174, 264. See also names of churches and denominations
Republican Party, 121, 130, 138, 145
Revolution, American, 41, 70, 71, 74
Reynolds, Joshua, 74
Riggs, Elisha Francis, 223
Riggs, George Washington, 222
Riggs Mill, 79
Ring tournament, 221, 261
Ritchie, 178
Riverdale, 191, 197, 201, 230, 259
Riversdale plantation, 86, 87, 91, 114, 115, 136, 142, 151, 198

River View, 147
Rogers family, 78, 179
Rogers, James Harris, 179
Rogers, John, 41
Roosevelt, Franklin D., 73, 212, 214, 227, 231
Rose Mount, 102
Rossborough Inn, 89, 122
Ross House, 162
Route One, 89, 182, 193, 196, 199, 228, 229, 240
Roziers Bluff, 121

S
Sacred Heart Church, 53
Sadler, Robert H., Jr., 107, 168, 169, 171
St. Barnabas Church, 67, 69
St. Ignatius Catholic Church, 146
St. John's Church, 185
St. Paul's Church, 51
St. Thomas Church, 52
Salubria, 105
Sasscer family, 49, 165
Sasscer, Lansdale G., 231
Savage, Edward, 80
Scholfield brothers, 79
School busing, 241, 249
Schools, 105, 137, 154, 193, 208, 218, 219, 241, 248, 249, 256, 257, 267
Science, 60, 250
Scottish immigrants, 31, 34, 47, 50, 61, 88
Scott, Henry T., 111
Seabrook, 143, 192
Seat Pleasant, 92, 157, 192, 206, 231, 243
Servants, indentured, 38, 55
Sewall family, 66
Shannon, J. Harry, 56, 70, 117, 155, 166, 171, 178
Sheriff, 28, 61, 266
Ship Ballast House, 56
Silesia, 137
Slaves, 28, 38, 39, 43, 55, 105, 116, 117, 121, 122, 128, 141
Smith, Capt. John, 15
Smith house (Riverdale), 197
Snowden family, 73, 87, 108, 122
Soest, Gerard, 21
Spa City, 190
Spa Spring, 161
Sprigg, Osborn, 68, 141
Sprigg, Samuel, 86, 100, 141
Sri Siva Vishnu Temple, 264
Stapko, Gregory, 58
Steamboats, 106, 140, 148, 157
Stier family, 91
Stoddert, Benjamin, 78, 86, 92, 97

Stoddert children, 79
Stuart, Gilbert, 91
Suitland, 138, 193, 212, 237
Suit, Samuel Taylor, 138
Surratt, Mary, 132, 133
Surrattsville, 133
Susquehannock Indians, 22, 28
Swift, John, 164

T
Takoma Park, 192, 195
Talbot, Anne, 66
Tasker, Col. Benjamin, 59
Tasker family, 56, 58, 59, 78
Tatham, William, 45
Tayac, Turkey, 235
Telegraph, 87
Temple Hills, 193
Three Sisters, 136
Tobacco, 11, 20, 38, 42, 88, 106, 115, 136, 138, 140; auctions, 167, 225, 263; photos, 43, 45, 83, 165, 167, 186, 225, 244, 262; warehouses, 40, 56, 102, 263
Totten, George Oakley, Jr., 222
Townsend, George Alfred, 138
Tricentennial, 248, 266–270
Trinity Episcopal Church, 110
Trueman's Point, 181
Tugwell, Rexford G., 214
Turkey Flight, 70
Turkeys, 225, 232
Turner, Albert, 237
Turner, Shadrick, 53
Turnpike, 87, 89, 95, 196

U
University of Maryland, 86, 89, 122, 151, 152, 182, 198, 226, 236, 240, 248, 262
Upper Gisboro, 130
Upper Marlboro, 53, 60, 71, 87, 94, 99, 110, 121, 138–140, 248; history, 31, 39, 43, 47; houses, 46, 47, 49, 76, 77, 100, 111, 113, 253, 254; scenes, 103, 110, 150, 157, 170, 178, 180, 183, 224, 243, 244, 260, 261, 266, 269, 270

V
Vansville, 87, 89
Vietnam War, 233, 240
Vietnamese immigrants, 248
Villa de Sales, 144

W
Wailes family, 99
Walker Mill, 178
Wallace, George C., 241
Warburton Manor, 46, 74, 81, 103

Wardrop-Buck House, 113
Waring family, 46, 138
War of 1812, 46, 87, 88, 94–99, 103, 129, 162, 267
Washington, Baltimore & Annapolis Railway, 192, 207
Washington, D.C., 40, 80–83, 94–99, 129, 130, 133, 149, 190, 194, 213, 228, 248
Washington, George, 46, 64, 69, 73, 74, 80, 103, 160; house, 175
Washington Redskins, 271
Washington, Spa Spring & Gretta Railroad, 205
Washington Suburban Sanitary Commission, 205
Waud, Alfred R., 128
Weems family, 184
Weems Line, 140
Welles, Sumner, 227
Weston, 100
West, Stephen, 41
Westwood, 163
Wheatley, H. Winship, Jr., 237
Whig Party, 88
Whitefield, George, 53
Whitemarsh, 53, 183
Wilfong, James C., Jr., 47, 112, 222
Wilkinson, Perry O., 231
Williams Plains, 111
Wilson, George, 129
Wilson, House, 47
Wilson's Station, 145
Wilson, Woodrow, 73
Wirt, William, 86, 104, 175
Wollaston, John, 56, 58, 63, 64
Women's rights, 145, 173
Wood, Thomas, 106
Woodville, See Aquasco
Woodward, William, Sr., 220
Woodyard, The, 30, 33, 41, 139
World War I, 180, 203
World War II, 230, 233
Wright brothers, 173

Y
Young, George Washington, 130

Z
Zantzinger, O. B., 207

Alan Virta grew up in Prince George's County and graduated from the University of Maryland with degrees in history and library science. He has researched and written on local history for the Prince George's County Historical Society since 1974 and served as the first chairman of the Prince George's County Historic Preservation Commission from 1982 to 1986. A certified archivist, he worked for the Library of Congress for twelve years and spent a year on an archival fellowship at the University of Southern Mississippi. Since 1988 he has been head of special collections and university archivist at Boise State University in Idaho.

5552918

1/01 - 10
7/02 - 20
7/03 - 25
3/05 - 33 (√6/05)
4/06 - 37 (√5/06)
11/07 - 3(12/07)